David H. Levin

Chess Master and Teacher

Syllogism Press
1070-E Highway 34
Suite 141
Matawan, NJ 07747
(908) 290-7901

First Printing: November 1994

Typeset using Microsoft® WORD for Windows™ software
Diagrams created using DIAGRAM 2.03 software

ISBN 0-9638001-1-6
Printed in the United States of America

CONTENTS

Children and Chess

To children, chess is a challenging and enjoyable pursuit. To parents and educators, chess is also a way to help a child develop patience, self-esteem, logical thinking skills, and the ability to concentrate.

About this Book

This book is primarily for children who are just learning the game of chess. The author presumes only that the child knows the rules for how chessmen move.

To avoid confusion, the puzzles, hints, and answers are stated as clearly and simply as possible. Chess notation is not used, since it could be a potential source of frustration. Technical terms are avoided where possible. The few terms that do appear are explained in a section called "About the Puzzles."

Puzzles featuring similar pieces appear in sequence, and in order of increasing difficulty. Ten of the most challenging puzzles appear at the end.

Acknowledgements

My thanks go to David Pfeffer and Justin Thorpe for trying out the puzzles and giving me a lot of ideas for improving them.

About the Puzzles

If a puzzle is hard to understand, this section can help.

First, here are rules for how the puzzles work:

1. White and Black take turns moving as in regular chess.

2. White pawns always move up the board, toward the top of the page.

3. Black pawns always move down the board, toward the bottom of the page.

4. White and Black each try their best in all of the puzzles.

Here is how the chessmen are shown in the puzzles, along with how they compare in value:

 **king** - more than all the other chessmen put together (you have to avoid checkmate no matter what!)

 **queen** - 9 points

 **knight** - 3 points

 **rook** - 5 points

 **pawn** - 1 point

 **bishop** - 3 points

Knowing how the chessmen compare helps you figure out which side is ahead in a chess game.

Here are some terms that are used in the puzzles:

take - means the same as capture, as in "bishop takes pawn."

win at least a pawn - capture a pawn for free, or make a trade that gains you 1 or more points altogether.

Example: trading a bishop for the opponent's rook would gain you two points.

Example: trading your pawn for the opponent's pawn would not gain or lose.

sacrifice - make a losing trade on purpose, knowing that you will end up ahead in points or bring checkmate against the opponent. Be careful before you sacrifice!

pawn promotion - when your pawn reaches the other side of the board, you get to replace it with a queen, rook, bishop, or knight. You should choose the queen almost all the time, since that piece is worth 9 points. You are allowed to promote to a queen even if your original queen is still on the board.

promoted piece - this means the piece that a pawn gets replaced with when it reaches the other side of the board. In some of the puzzles, the other side promotes a pawn. Since we don't know what piece the opponent would pick, we just call it a "promoted piece."

promotion square - this is where a pawn will end up if it reaches the other side of the board.

queening square - what most people say when they really mean "promotion square." This is because pawns are almost always promoted to queens.

passed pawn - a pawn that can reach promotion unless one of the opponent's pieces can stop it. This is where the opponent doesn't have pawns that can do the job.

draw - a game that ends with no one winning or losing.

stalemate - where the side whose turn it is, has no legal move or capture, and its king is NOT in check. Stalemate counts as a draw.

PUZZLE #1

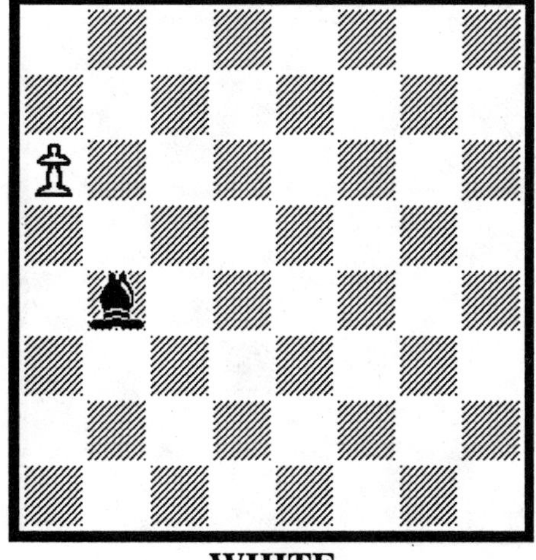

WHITE

It is Black's turn to move. White's pawn is only two squares from promoting. Where should Black's bishop go so that it can capture White's pawn before it promotes?

Confused? Read "About the Puzzles" starting on page 2.

Answer on page 95

PUZZLE #2

BLACK

WHITE

It is Black's turn to move. White's pawn is about to promote. Where should Black's bishop move so that it can capture the promoted piece? There are two answers, can you find both?

Confused? Read "About the Puzzles" starting on page 2.

Answer on page 96

PUZZLE #3

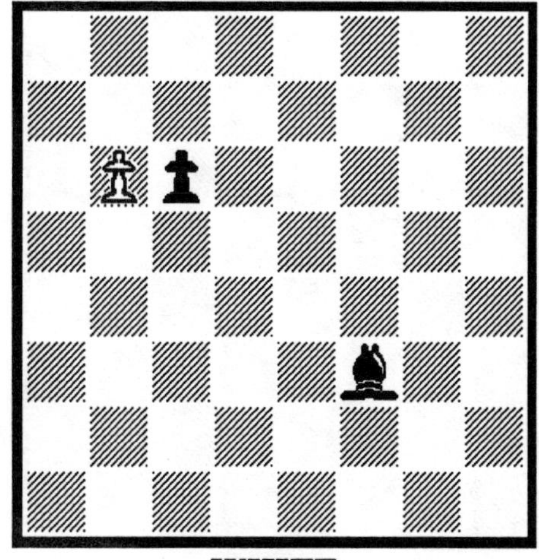

WHITE

It is Black's turn to move. White's pawn is ready to advance and promote. What move will enable Black's bishop to capture White's pawn before it promotes?

Confused? Read "About the Puzzles" starting on page 2.

Answer on page 97

PUZZLE #4

It is Black's turn to move. One of White's pawns can promote in three moves. Where should Black's bishop move so that it can capture White's passed pawn before it promotes?

Don't read the hint until you've tried your best.

Answer on page 98

(Hint: Try to control the light square in front of White's passed pawn.)

PUZZLE #5

BLACK

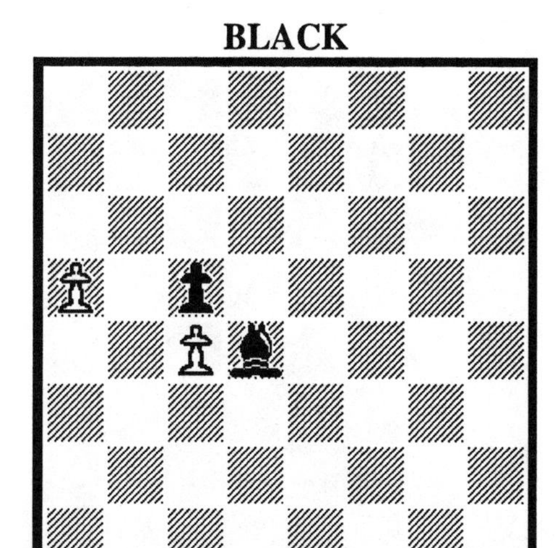

WHITE

It is Black's turn to move. One of White's pawns can promote in three moves. Where should Black's bishop move so that it can capture White's passed pawn before it promotes?

Don't read the hint until you've tried your best.

Answer on page 99

(Hint: Try to control the dark square in front of White's passed pawn.)

PUZZLE #6

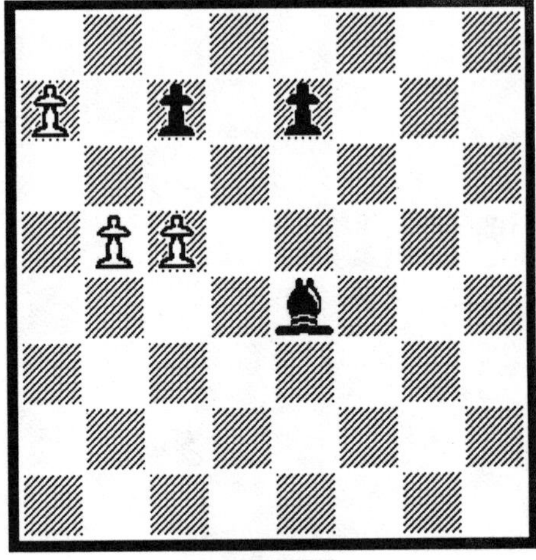

It is White's turn to move. White has a pawn that is only one square from promoting. But if it promotes now, Black's bishop could take it. What move will enable White's pawn to promote without being captured?

Don't read the hint until you've tried your best.

Answer on page 100

(Hint: Try to block the bishop from controlling the promotion square.)

PUZZLE #7

It is White's turn to move. Black's bishop makes it hard to promote a pawn. But White can still do it. How?

Don't read the hint until you've tried your best.

Answer on page 101

(Hint: Look for a sacrifice.)

PUZZLE #8

WHITE

It is White's turn to move. Both White pawns are only two squares from promotion. How does White promote a pawn so that Black's bishop can't capture it?

Don't read the hint until you've tried your best.

Answer on page 102

(Hint: Look for a sacrifice.)

PUZZLE #9

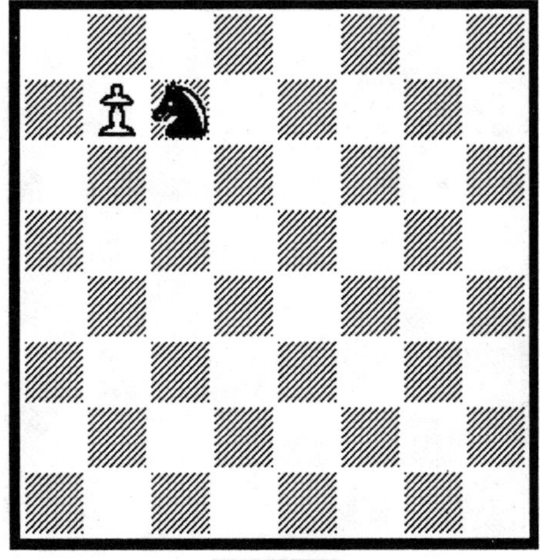

WHITE

It is Black's turn to move. White's pawn is about to promote. Where should Black's knight move so that it can capture the promoted piece?

Confused? Read "About the Puzzles" starting on page 2.

Answer on page 103

PUZZLE #10

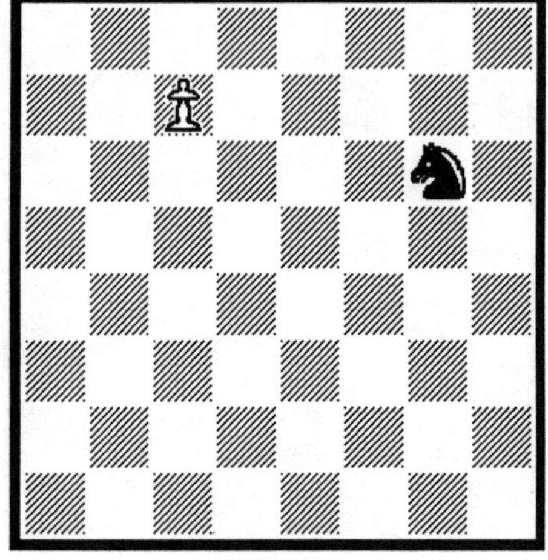

WHITE

It is Black's turn to move. White's pawn is about to promote. Where should Black's knight move so that it can capture the promoted piece?

Confused? Read "About the Puzzles" starting on page 2.

Answer on page 104

PUZZLE #11

WHITE

It is Black's turn to move. White has two advanced pawns, but Black's knight has a move that allows it to capture one pawn before it promotes, and the other pawn right after it promotes. Where should the knight move?

Confused? Read "About the Puzzles" starting on page 2.

Answer on page 105

PUZZLE #12

WHITE

It is Black's turn to move. White has a pawn that is only two squares away from promoting. However, there is a way for Black's knight to block the passed pawn from promoting. Can you find it?

Confused? Read "About the Puzzles" starting on page 2.

Answer on page 106

PUZZLE #13

BLACK

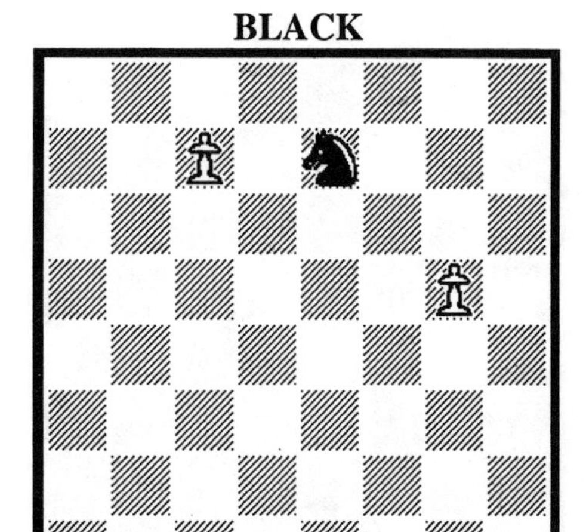

WHITE

It is White's turn to move. White has a way to promote a pawn so that Black's knight can't capture it. This takes a few moves. Can you see how?

Don't read the hint until you've tried your best.

Answer on page 107

(Hint: Look for a sacrifice.)

PUZZLE #14

WHITE

It is White's turn to move. There is a way for White to promote a pawn in two moves so that Black's knight can't capture the promoted piece. To do that, where should White move?

Confused? Read "About the Puzzles" starting on page 2.

Answer on page 108

PUZZLE #15

BLACK

WHITE

It is White's turn to move. There is a way for White to promote a pawn in a few moves so that Black's knight can't do anything about it. Where should White move?

Confused? Read "About the Puzzles" starting on page 2.

Answer on page 109

PUZZLE #16

It is Black's turn to move. White's pawn is only two squares away from promoting. However, there is a way for Black to move so that the knight could capture the promoted piece. What should be Black's next two moves?

Don't read the hint until you've tried your best.

Answer on page 110

(Hint: What move would you make if Black's pawn were somewhere else? Now go back to the actual puzzle.)

PUZZLE #17

BLACK

WHITE

It is Black's turn to move. White has a pawn only two squares away from promoting. However, there is one way for Black to move so that the knight could capture the promoted piece. How?

Don't read the hint until you've tried your best.

Answer on page 111

(Hint: What move would you make if Black's pawn were somewhere else? Now go back to the actual puzzle.)

PUZZLE #18

BLACK

WHITE

It is Black's turn to move. White's pawn is only two squares away from promoting. However, there is one way for Black's knight to get back in time to capture the promoted piece. How?

Confused? Read "About the Puzzles" starting on page 2.

Answer on page 112

PUZZLE #19

BLACK

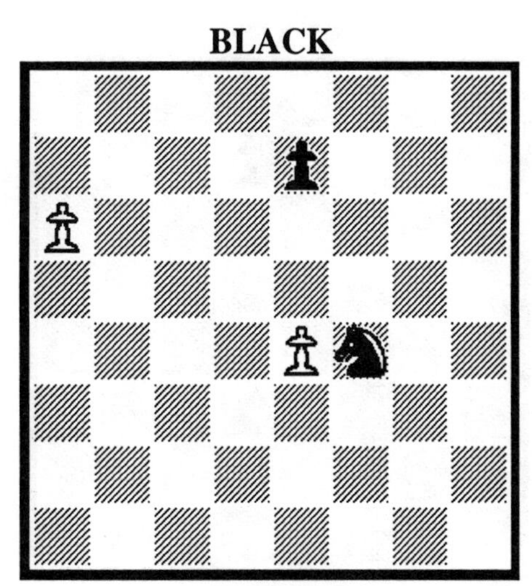

WHITE

It is Black's turn to move. White has a pawn only two squares away from promoting. However, there is one way for Black's knight to get back in time to capture the promoted piece. How?

Confused? Read "About the Puzzles" starting on page 2.

Answer on page 113

PUZZLE #20

It is Black's turn to move. White has a pawn that is only two squares away from promoting. However, there is one way for Black's knight to get back in time to capture the promoted piece. How?

Confused? Read "About the Puzzles" starting on page 2.

Answer on page 114

PUZZLE #21

It is White's turn to move. There is a move that leads to the capture of Black's knight. What is it?

Don't read the hint until you've tried your best.

Answer on page 115

(Hint: Use White's pawns to control all the places the knight could move.)

PUZZLE #22

BLACK

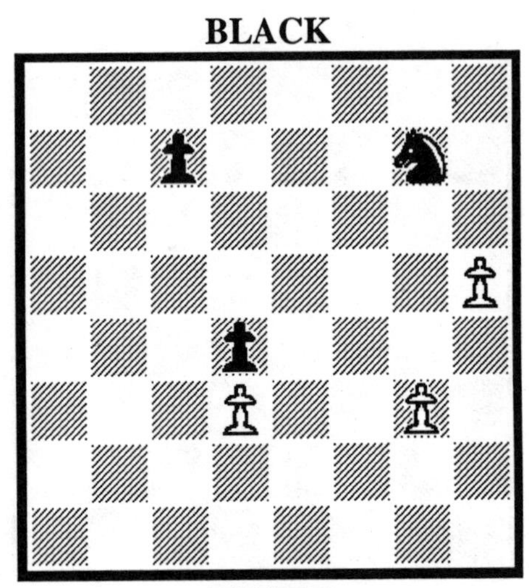

WHITE

It is White's turn to move. White has a way to safely promote a pawn in a few moves. What move should White play?

Confused? Read "About the Puzzles" starting on page 2.

Answer on page 116

PUZZLE #23

BLACK

WHITE

It is White's turn to move. How does White promote a pawn so that Black's rook can not capture the promoted piece?

Don't read the hint until you've tried your best.

Answer on page 117

(Hint: Look for a sacrifice.)

PUZZLE #24

It is White's turn to move. There is a way for White to promote a pawn so that Black's rook can't capture the promoted piece. This takes several moves. How does White do it?

Confused? Read "About the Puzzles" starting on page 2.

Answer on page 118

PUZZLE #25

BLACK

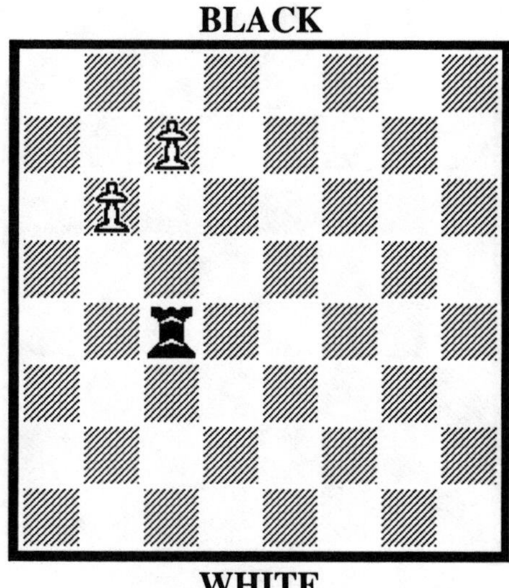

WHITE

It is White's turn to move. There is a way for White to promote a pawn in a few moves so that Black's rook can't capture the promoted piece. How?

Don't read the hint until you've tried your best.

Answer on page 119

(Hint: Look for a sacrifice.)

PUZZLE #26

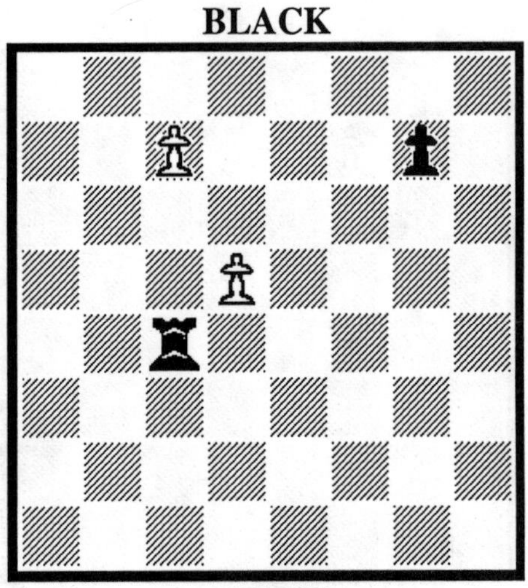

It is White's turn to move. There is a way for White to promote a pawn so that Black's rook can't capture the promoted piece. This takes several moves. How does White do it?

Don't read the hint until you've tried your best.

Answer on page 120

(Hint: Think of the previous puzzle.)

PUZZLE #27

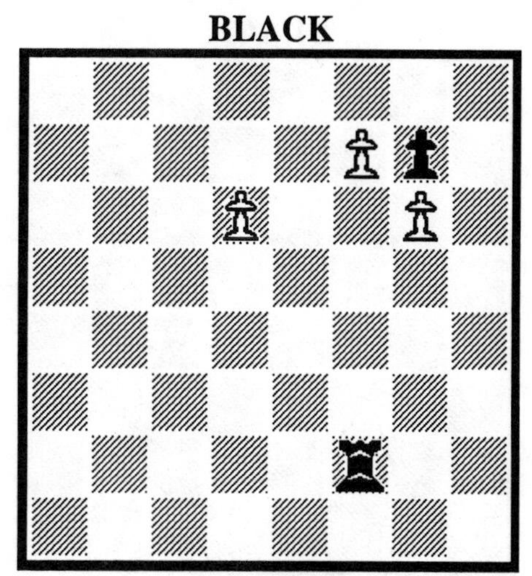

WHITE

It is White's turn to move. White has two pawns that are close to promoting. How can White promote in a few moves so that Black's rook can't capture the promoted piece?

Confused? Read "About the Puzzles" starting on page 2.

Answer on page 121

PUZZLE #28

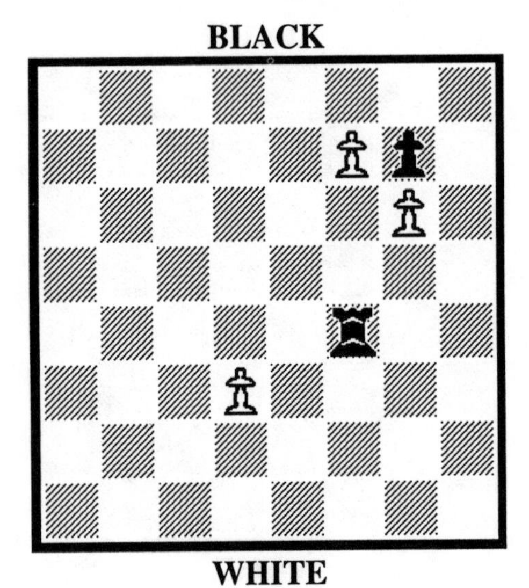

It is White's turn to move. There is a way for White to promote a pawn so that Black's rook can't capture it. This takes many moves. How does White do it?

Don't read the hint until you've tried your best.

Answer on page 122

(Hint: Look for a sacrifice.)

PUZZLE #29

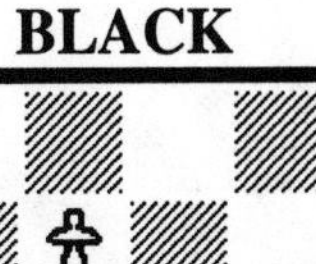

BLACK

WHITE

It is Black's turn to move. White has two pawns that are close to promoting. Where should Black's rook move so that it could capture any White promoted piece?

Confused? Read "About the Puzzles" starting on page 2.

Answer on page 123

PUZZLE #30

It is Black's turn to move. A White pawn is about to promote. Where does Black move so that White's promoted piece could be captured?

Confused? Read "About the Puzzles" starting on page 2.

Answer on page 124

PUZZLE #31

WHITE

It is Black's turn to move. White has a pawn that is only two moves from promoting. Black's rook needs to move so that it could capture the promoted piece. How?

Don't read the hint until you've tried your best.

Answer on page 95

(Hint: Find a way to get the rook "behind" the pawn.)

PUZZLE #32

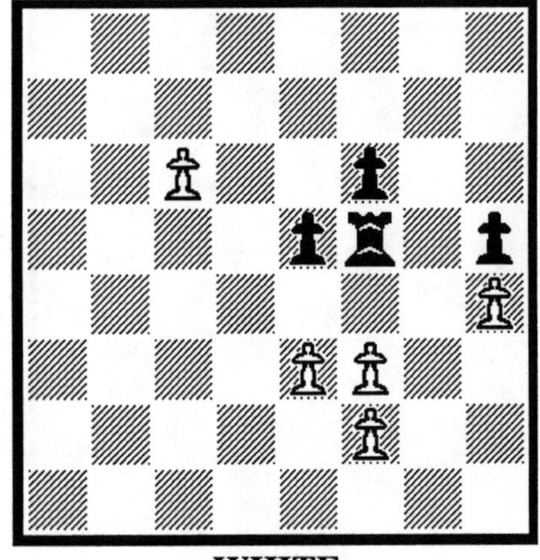

WHITE

It is Black's turn to move. White has a pawn that is only two moves from promoting. There is only one way for Black's rook to be ready to capture the promoted piece. Can you find it?

Don't read the hint until you've tried your best.

Answer on page 96

(Hint: Find a way to get the rook "behind" the pawn.)

PUZZLE #33

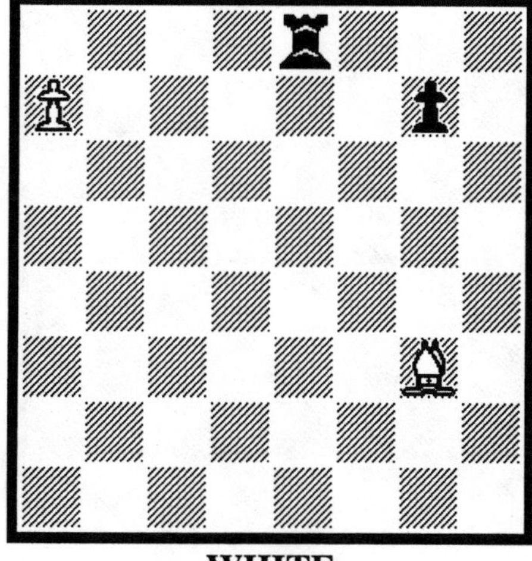

WHITE

It is White's turn to move. White's pawn is only one square from promotion. White has a move that enables the pawn to promote so that Black's rook can't take it. Can you find it?

Don't read the hint until you've tried your best.

Answer on page 97

(Hint: Find a way to block the rook from the promotion square.)

PUZZLE #34

BLACK

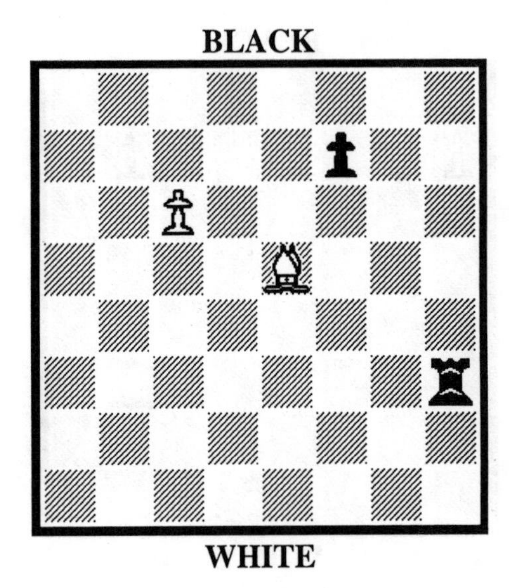

WHITE

It is White's turn to move. White's pawn is only two squares from promotion. How does White promote the pawn so that Black's rook has no way to capture the promoted piece?

Confused? Read "About the Puzzles" starting on page 2.

Answer on page 98

PUZZLE #35

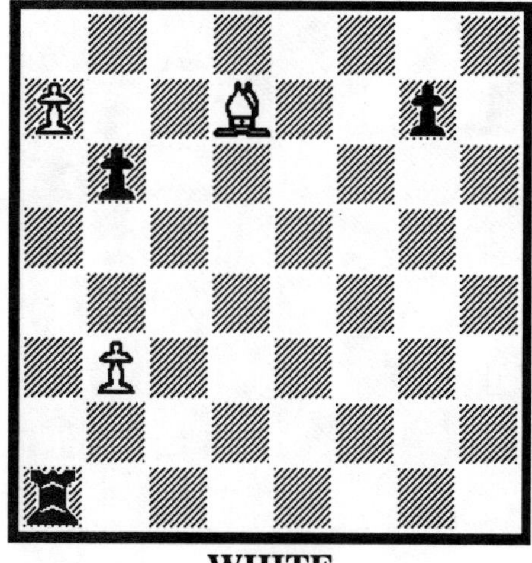

WHITE

It is White's turn to move. White has a pawn only one square from promotion. How does White get ready to promote the pawn so that Black's rook has no way to capture the promoted piece?

Don't read the hint until you've tried your best.

Answer on page 99

(Hint: Find a way to block the rook.)

PUZZLE #36

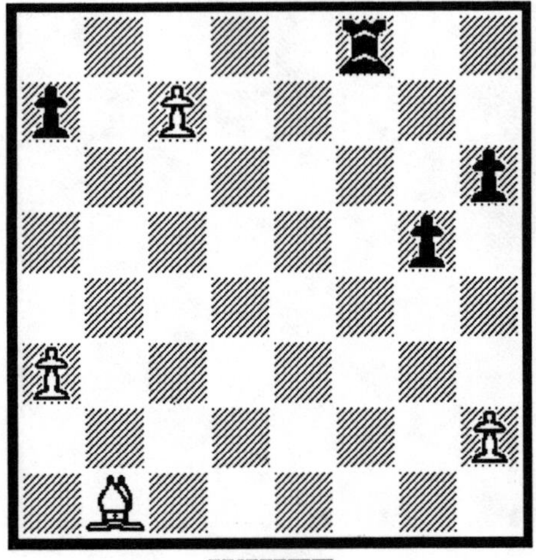

WHITE

It is White's turn to move. If White's advanced pawn were to promote right now, the promoted piece could be taken by Black's rook. But White has a way to control the promoting square and then promote, so that "rook takes queen" allows White to take the rook. What should White play?

Don't read the hint until you've tried your best.

Answer on page 100

(Hint: Use the bishop to control the promoting square.)

PUZZLE #37

BLACK

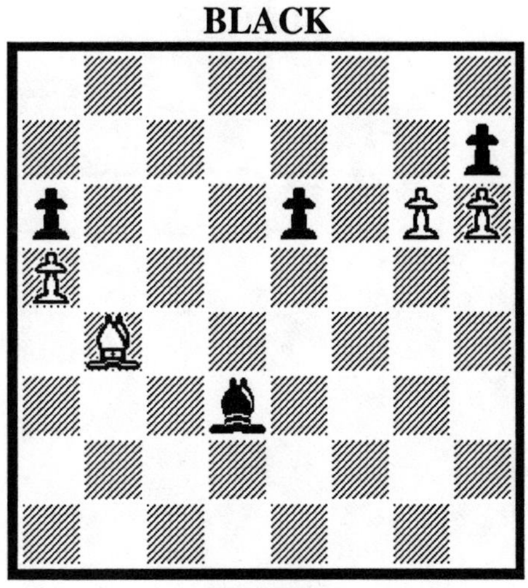

WHITE

It is White's turn to move. White can promote a pawn in two moves. Do you see how?

Confused? Read "About the Puzzles" starting on page 2.

Answer on page 101

PUZZLE #38

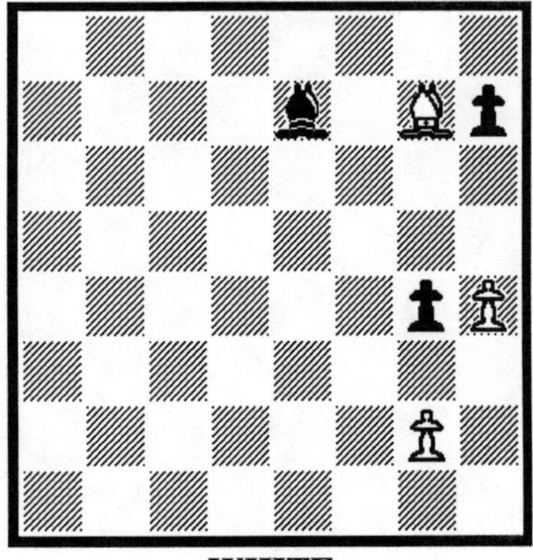

WHITE

It is Black's turn to move. Black has a move to safely capture a White pawn. How?

Confused? Read "About the Puzzles" starting on page 2.

Answer on page 102

PUZZLE #39

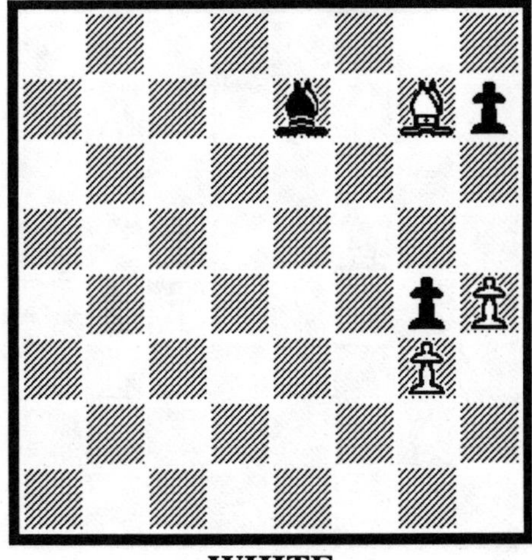

WHITE

It is Black's turn to move. Black has a move that gets ready to safely capture a White pawn without Black's man being captured. What is the move?

Confused? Read "About the Puzzles" starting on page 2.

Answer on page 103

PUZZLE #40

BLACK

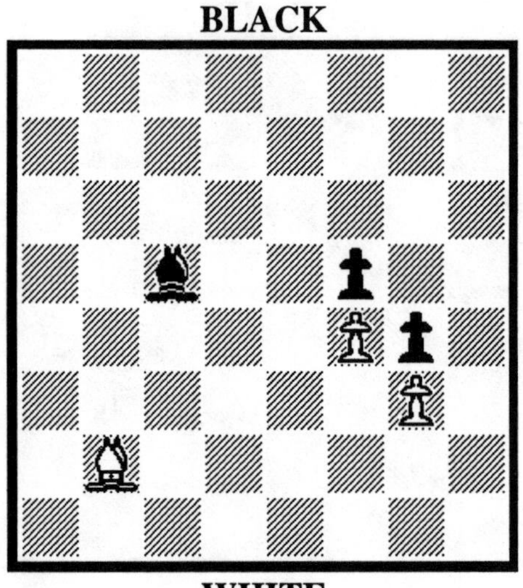

WHITE

It is Black's turn to move. Black has a move that gets ready to safely capture a White pawn, without Black's man being captured. What is the move?

Confused? Read "About the Puzzles" starting on page 2.

Answer on page 104

PUZZLE #41

BLACK

WHITE

It is Black's turn to move. "Bishop takes pawn" is not good because White plays "bishop takes bishop." But Black has a move that gets ready to safely capture that White pawn. What is the move?

Don't read the hint until you've tried your best.

Answer on page 105

(Hint: Keep attacking the pawn.)

PUZZLE #42

BLACK

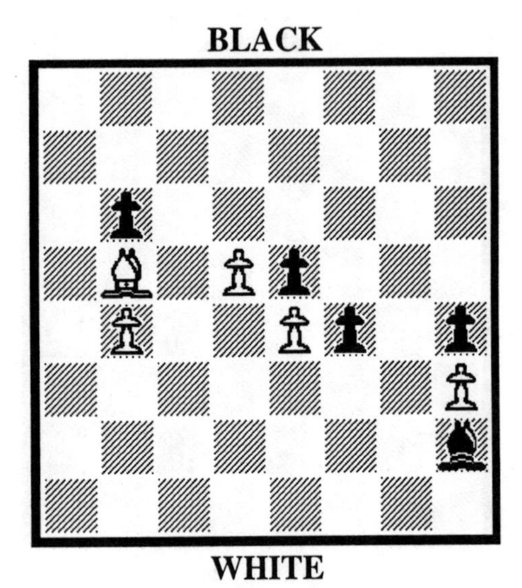

WHITE

It is Black's turn to move. White has a pawn only three squares from promoting. Yet that is just enough time for Black's bishop to get in position to capture the promoted piece. How?

Don't read the hint until you've tried your best.

Answer on page 106

(Hint: Black should move a pawn to make room for the bishop.)

PUZZLE #43

It is Black's turn to move. White's knight is attacking two Black pawns. Black has only one move to stop White from taking a pawn for free. What is it?

Don't read the hint until you've tried your best.

Answer on page 107

(Hint: Black's bishop cannot protect both Black pawns.)

PUZZLE #44

BLACK

WHITE

It is White's turn to move. White has a way to win a pawn no matter how Black answers. What move should White play?

Don't read the hint until you've tried your best.

Answer on page 108

(Hint: Find a way to attack two pawns at once.)

PUZZLE #45

WHITE

It is Black's turn to move. Black has a way to win a pawn no matter how White answers. What move should Black play?

Don't read the hint until you've tried your best.

Answer on page 109

(Hint: Find a way to attack two pawns at once.)

PUZZLE #46

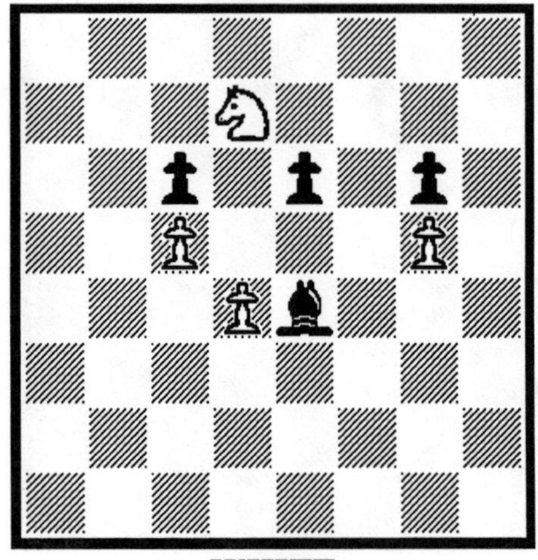

WHITE

It is White's turn to move. White has a way to win a pawn no matter how Black answers. What move should White play?

Don't read the hint until you've tried your best.

Answer on page 110

(Hint: Notice that Black's bishop now protects two Black pawns. If the bishop moved, one of those pawns would be unprotected.)

PUZZLE #47

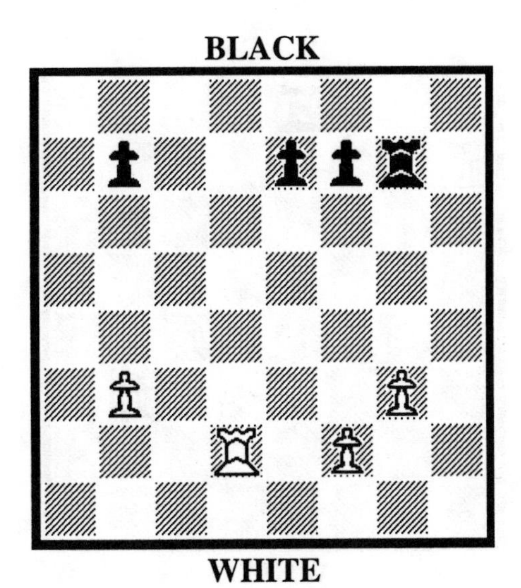

It is White's turn to move. White has a way to win a pawn no matter what Black does. What move should White play?

Don't read the hint until you've tried your best.

Answer on page 111

(Hint: Find a way for White to attack two Black pawns.)

PUZZLE #48

It is White's turn to move. White has a way to win at least a pawn no matter what Black does. What move should White play?

Don't read the hint until you've tried your best.

Answer on page 112

(Hint: Notice that Black's rook needs to control the promotion square of White's advanced pawn.)

PUZZLE #49

BLACK

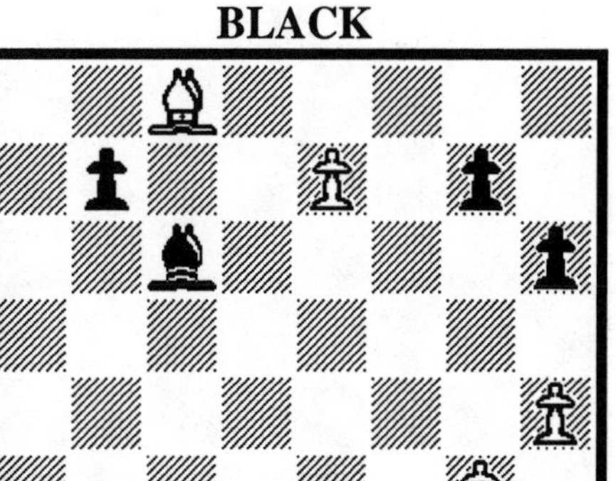

WHITE

It is White's turn to move. White has a way to win at least a pawn no matter what Black does. What move should White play?

Don't read the hint until you've tried your best.

Answer on page 113

(Hint: Notice that Black's bishop needs to control the promotion square of White's advanced pawn.)

PUZZLE #50

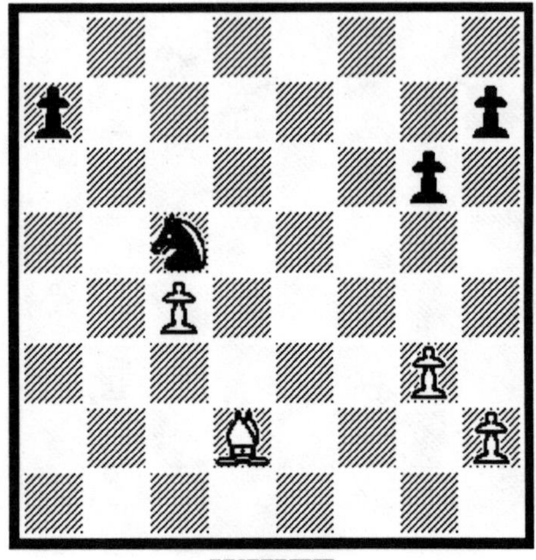

WHITE

It is White's turn to move. White has a way to win at least a pawn no matter what Black does. What move should White play?

Don't read the hint until you've tried your best.

Answer on page 114

(Hint: Notice how Black's knight is lined up with one of its pawns.)

PUZZLE #51

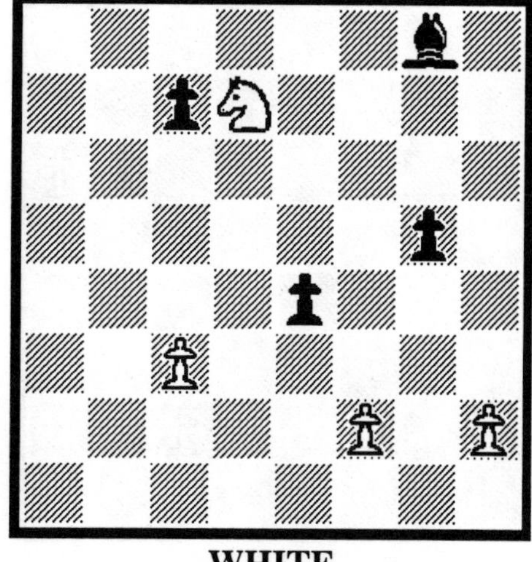

WHITE

It is White's turn to move. White has a way to win at least a pawn no matter what Black does. What move should White play?

Don't read the hint until you've tried your best.

Answer on page 115

(Hint: Find a way to attack two of Black's chessmen.)

PUZZLE #52

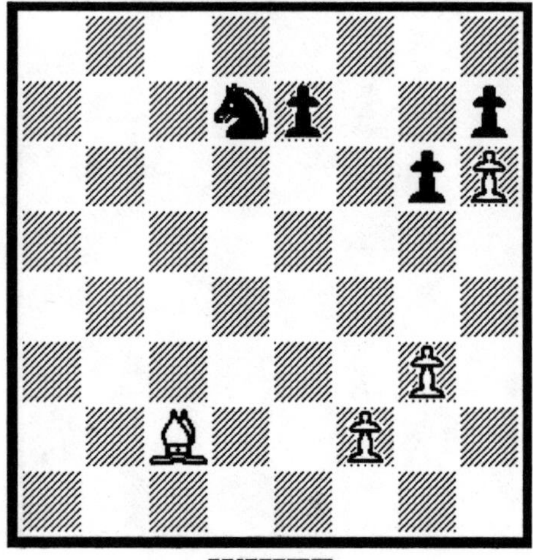

WHITE

It is White's turn to move. White has a way to win at least a pawn. How?

Don't read the hint until you've tried your best.

Answer on page 116

(Hint: Notice that White's advanced pawn would soon promote if Black's pawn wasn't in the way.)

PUZZLE #53

It is White's turn to move. White has a way to win Black's bishop. How?

Confused? Read "About the Puzzles" starting on page 2.

Answer on page 117

PUZZLE #54

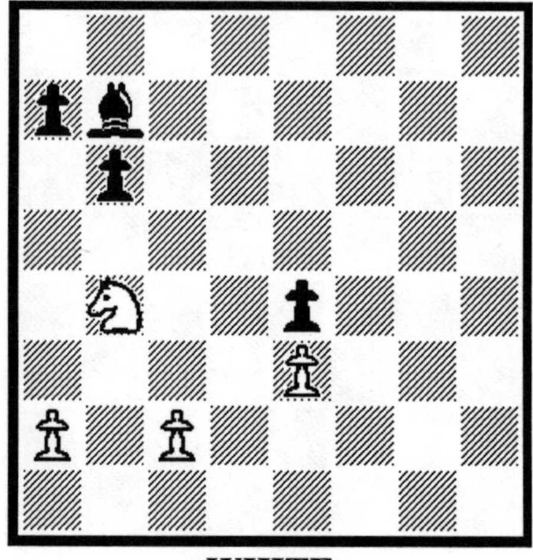

WHITE

It is Black's turn to move. Black has a way to win White's knight. How?

Don't read the hint until you've tried your best.

Answer on page 118

(Hint: Notice that wherever White's knight moves, Black can take it.)

PUZZLE #55

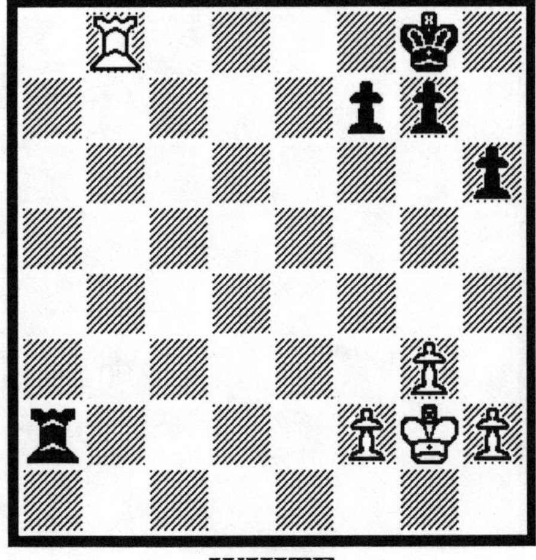

WHITE

It is Black's turn to move. White's rook has put Black's king in check. Black has only one way to get out of check. Can you find it?

Confused? Read "About the Puzzles" starting on page 2.

Answer on page 119

PUZZLE #56

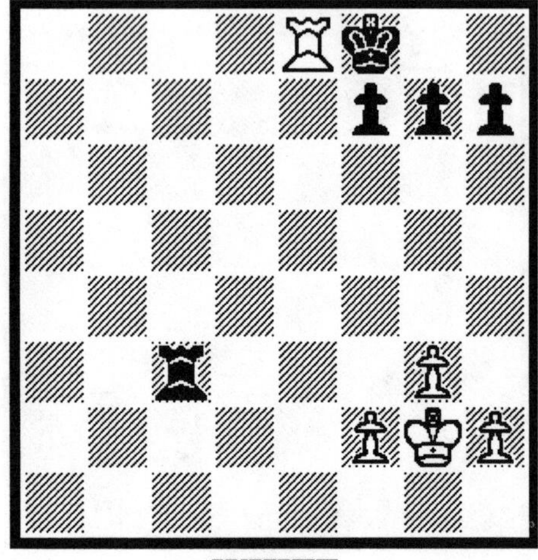

WHITE

It is Black's turn to move. White's rook has put Black's king in check. Black has only one way to get out of check. Can you find it?

Confused? Read "About the Puzzles" starting on page 2.

Answer on page 120

PUZZLE #57

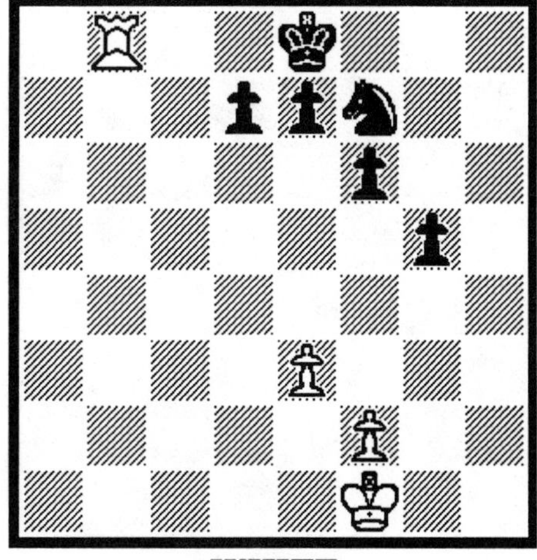

WHITE

It is Black's turn to move. White's rook has put Black's king in check. Black has only one way to get out of check. Can you find it?

Confused? Read "About the Puzzles" starting on page 2.

Answer on page 121

PUZZLE #58

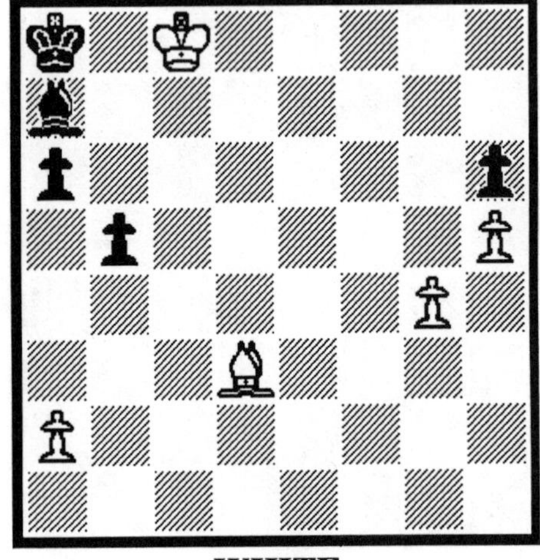

WHITE

It is White's turn to move. White can checkmate Black in one move. Can you find it?

Confused? Read "About the Puzzles" starting on page 2.

Answer on page 122

PUZZLE #59

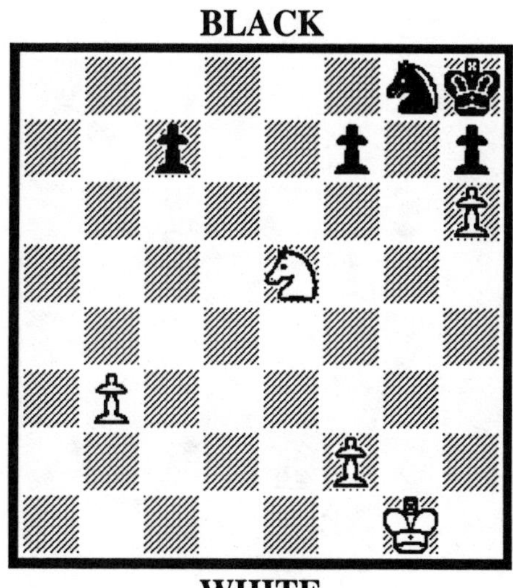

It is White's turn to move. White can checkmate Black in one move. Can you find it?

Confused? Read "About the Puzzles" starting on page 2.

Answer on page 123

PUZZLE #60

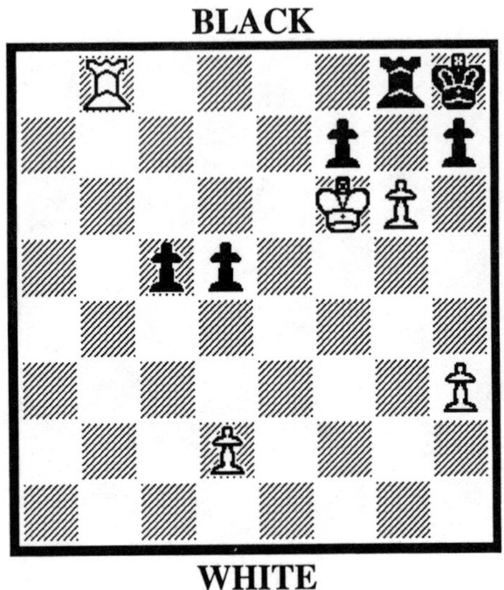

It is White's turn to move. White can checkmate Black in one move. Can you find it?

Confused? Read "About the Puzzles" starting on page 2.

Answer on page 124

PUZZLE #61

BLACK

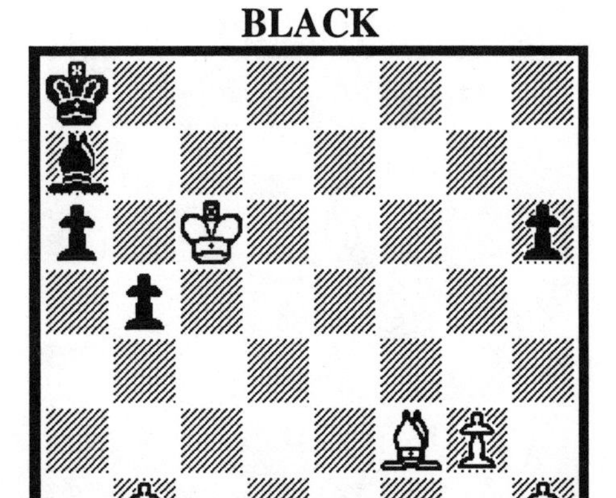

WHITE

It is White's turn to move. White can checkmate Black in one move. Can you find it?

Confused? Read "About the Puzzles" starting on page 2.

Answer on page 95

PUZZLE #62

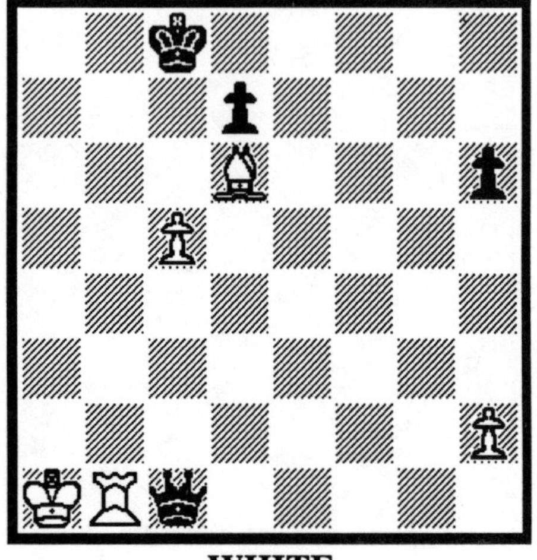

WHITE

It is Black's turn to move. Black can checkmate White in one move. Can you find it?

Confused? Read "About the Puzzles" starting on page 2.

Answer on page 96

PUZZLE #63

BLACK

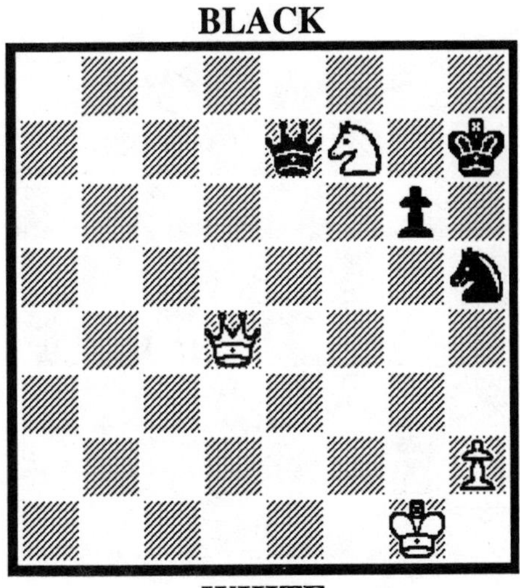

WHITE

It is White's turn to move. White can checkmate Black in one move. Can you find it?

Confused? Read "About the Puzzles" starting on page 2.

Answer on page 97

PUZZLE #64

BLACK

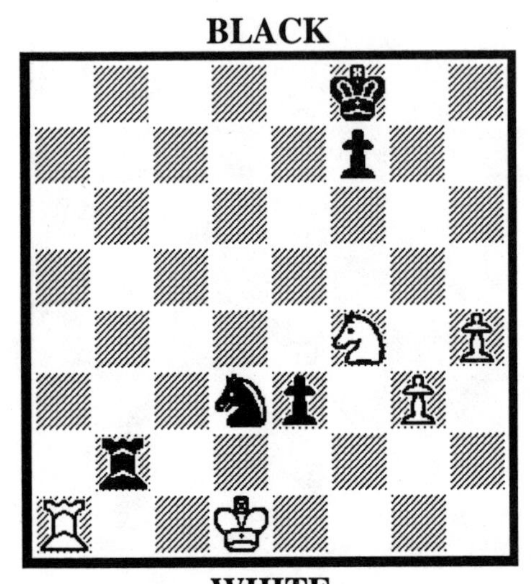

WHITE

It is Black's turn to move. Black can checkmate White in one move. Can you find it?

Confused? Read "About the Puzzles" starting on page 2.

Answer on page 98

PUZZLE #65

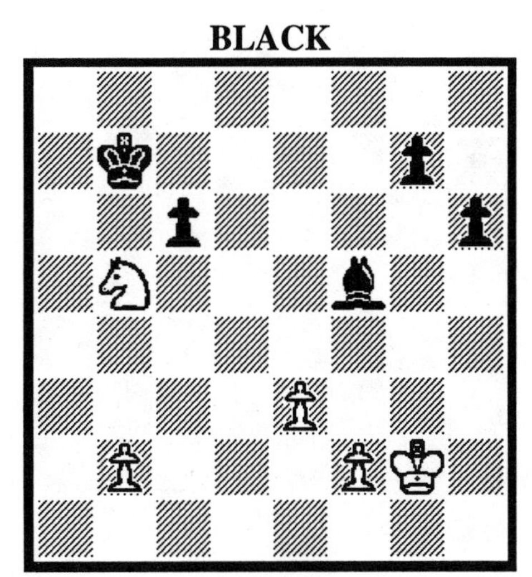

It is White's turn to move. White can win the Black bishop no matter what Black does. How?

Don't read the hint until you've tried your best.

Answer on page 99

(Hint: Look for a way to attack two pieces at once.)

PUZZLE #66

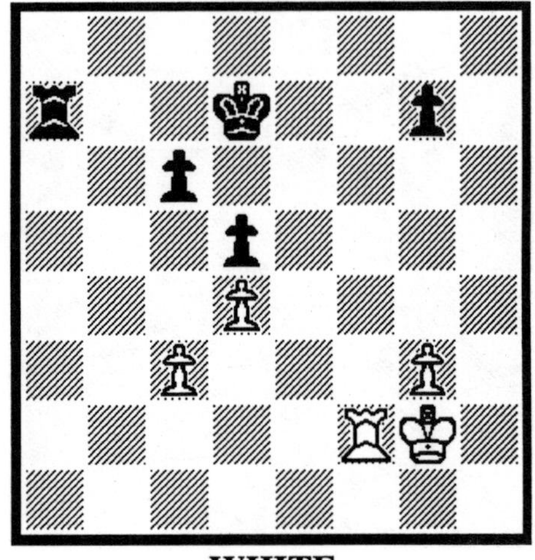

WHITE

It is White's turn to move. White can win the Black rook no matter what Black does. How?

Don't read the hint until you've tried your best.

Answer on page 100

(Hint: Notice how Black's king and rook are lined up.)

PUZZLE #67

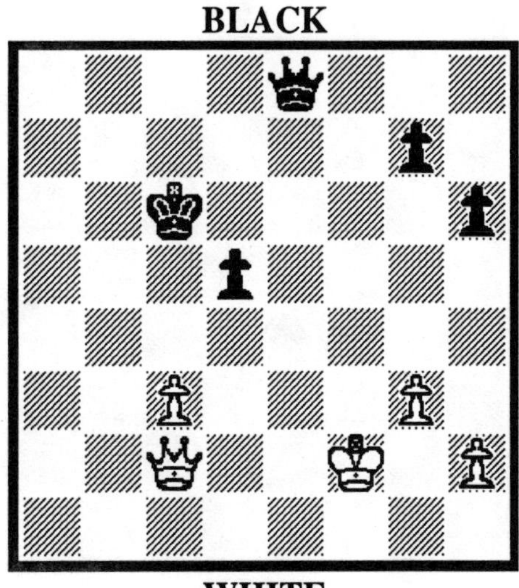

It is White's turn to move. White can win the Black queen no matter what Black does. How?

Don't read the hint until you've tried your best.

Answer on page 101

(Hint: Notice how Black's king and queen are lined up.)

PUZZLE #68

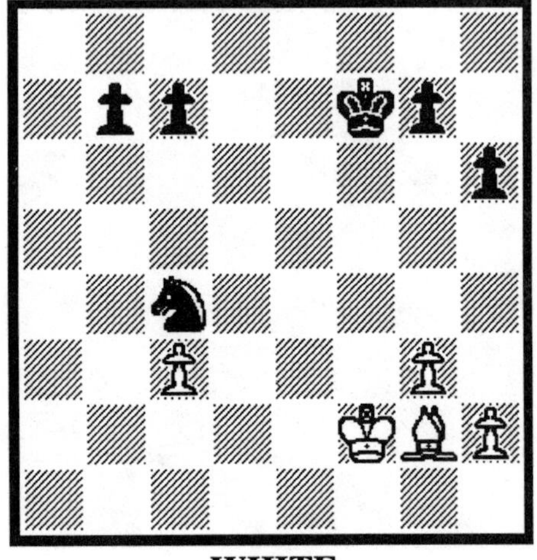

WHITE

It is White's turn to move. White can win the Black knight no matter what Black does. How?

Don't read the hint until you've tried your best.

Answer on page 102

(Hint: Notice how Black's king and knight are lined up.)

PUZZLE #69

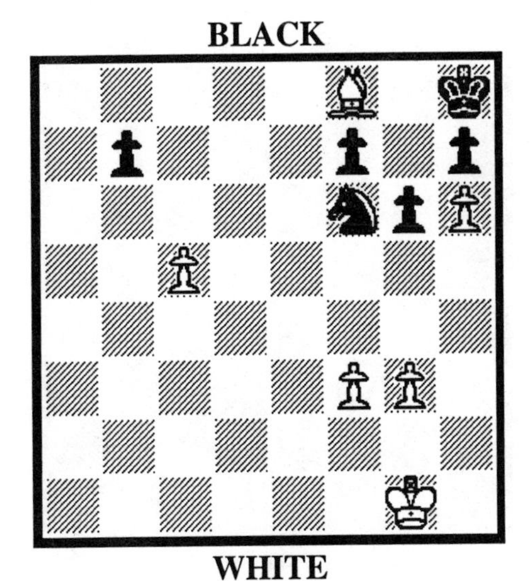

It is White's turn to move. White has a way to win Black's knight for free no matter what Black does. How?

Don't read the hint until you've tried your best.

Answer on page 103

(Hint: Notice how Black's king and knight are lined up.)

PUZZLE #70

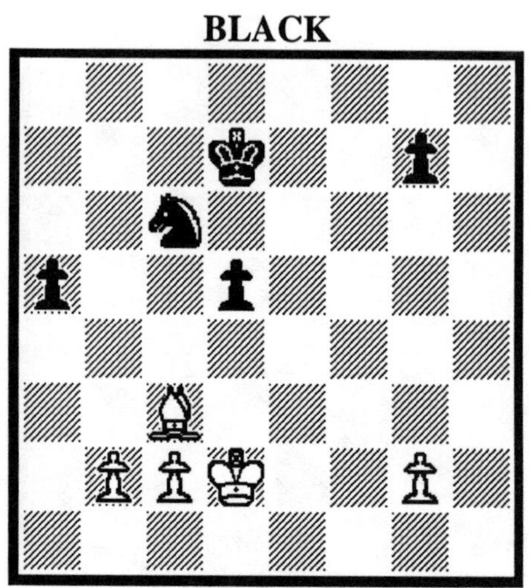

It is Black's turn to move. Black has a way to win the White bishop for a pawn, no matter what White does. How?

Confused? Read "About the Puzzles" starting on page 2.

Answer on page 104

PUZZLE #71

BLACK

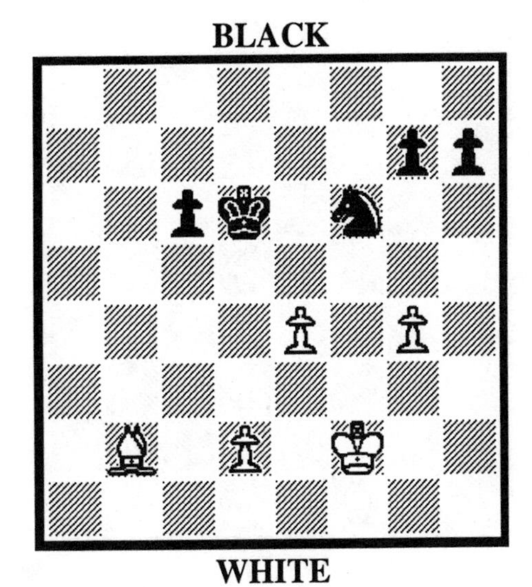

WHITE

It is White's turn to move. If White plays "bishop takes knight," Black has "pawn takes bishop." But White has a way to win the Black knight for a pawn, no matter what Black does. How?

Don't read the hint until you've tried your best.

Answer on page 105

(Hint: Try to attack two pieces at once.)

PUZZLE #72

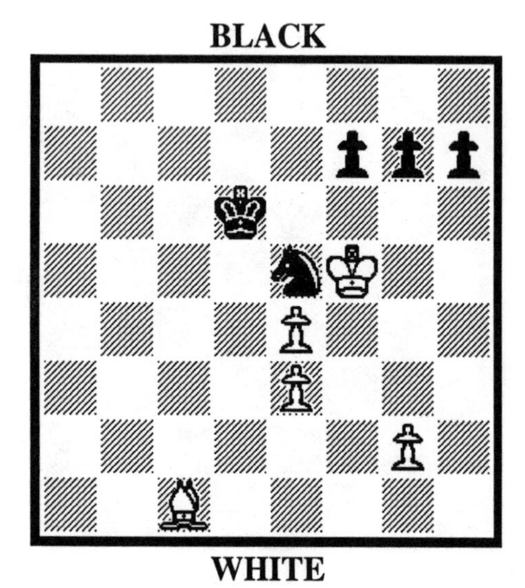

It is White's turn to move. White has a way to win the Black knight for free, no matter what Black does. How?

Don't read the hint until you've tried your best.

Answer on page 106

(Hint: Notice that Black's knight is protected only by its king.)

PUZZLE #73

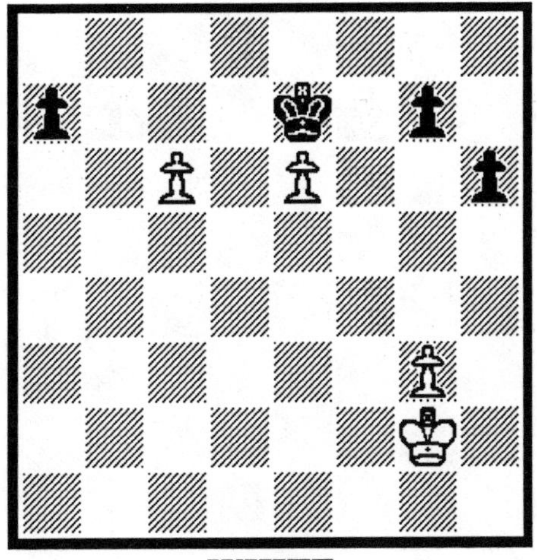

WHITE

It is White's turn to move. Black is ready to play "king takes pawn" and then go after White's other advanced pawn. But White has a way to promote a pawn in two moves so that Black can't capture the promoted piece. What move should White play?

Confused? Read "About the Puzzles" starting on page 2.

Answer on page 107

PUZZLE #74

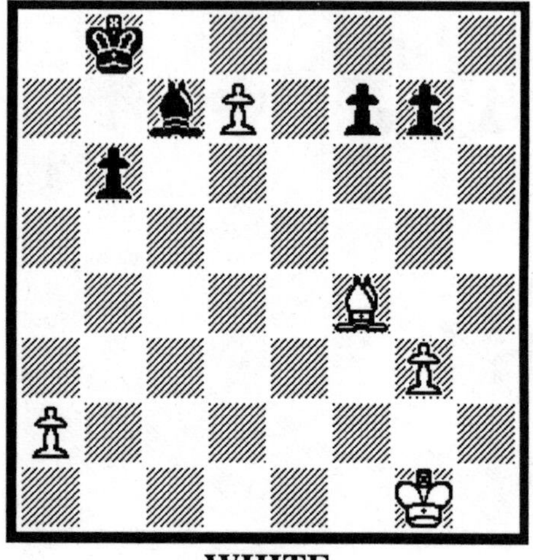

WHITE

It is White's turn to move. Black's bishop controls the promotion square of White's advanced pawn. Yet, White has a way to safely promote the pawn. How?

Confused? Read "About the Puzzles" starting on page 2.

Answer on page 108

PUZZLE #75

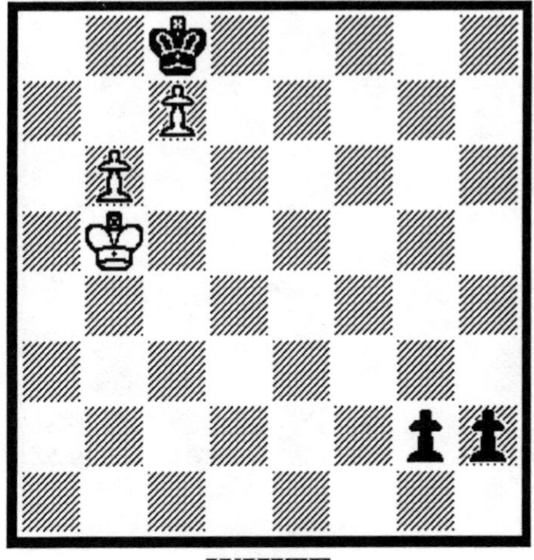

WHITE

It is White's turn to move. Black is about to promote a pawn, and White can't stop it. But White still wins the game. What should White's next two moves be?

Don't read the hint until you've tried your best.

Answer on page 109

(Hint: White can checkmate Black in two moves.)

PUZZLE #76

BLACK

WHITE

It is White's turn to move. White has a way to win Black's knight for free no matter what Black does. How?

Don't read the hint until you've tried your best.

Answer on page 110

(Hint: Try to force the Black knight to give itself up to save its king.)

PUZZLE #77

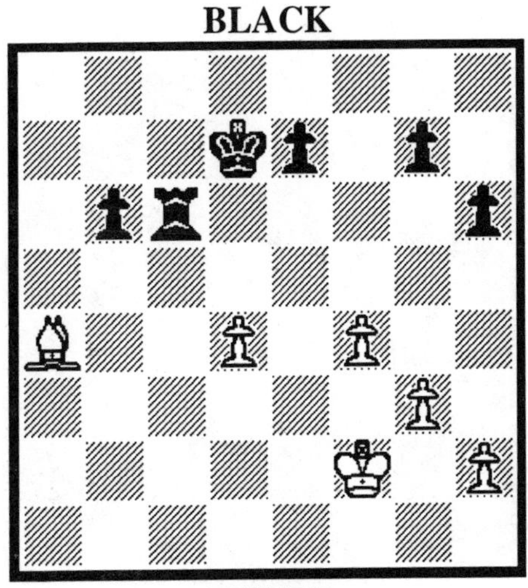

It is White's turn to move. White can play "bishop takes rook, check" but then Black can play "king takes bishop." There is a way for White to get ready to take the rook for free. How?

Don't read the hint until you've tried your best.

Answer on page 111

(Hint: Notice that the rook cannot move because that would put Black's king in check.)

PUZZLE #78

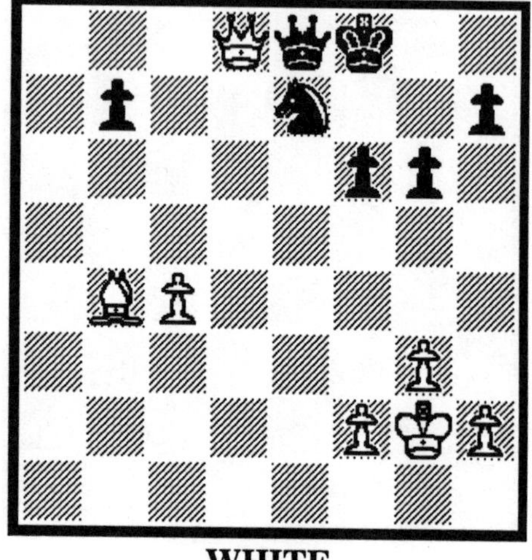

WHITE

It is White's turn to move. White has a way to capture the Black knight for free. Can you find it?

Don't read the hint until you've tried your best.

Answer on page 112

(Hint: Does Black's queen really protect the knight?)

PUZZLE #79

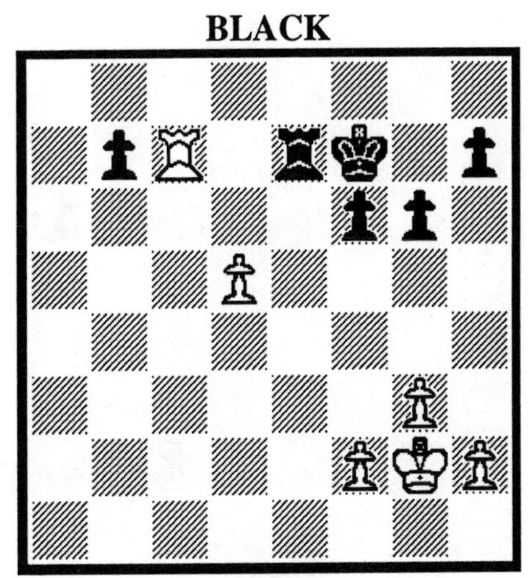

It is White's turn to move. Black's rook blocks its king from being in check. The Black rook also attacks White's rook. But White has a way to either win the Black rook for free, or put a White pawn only one square from promoting. What move should White make?

Don't read the hint until you've tried your best.

Answer on page 113

(Hint: Look for a way to attack the Black rook and also protect the White rook.)

PUZZLE #80

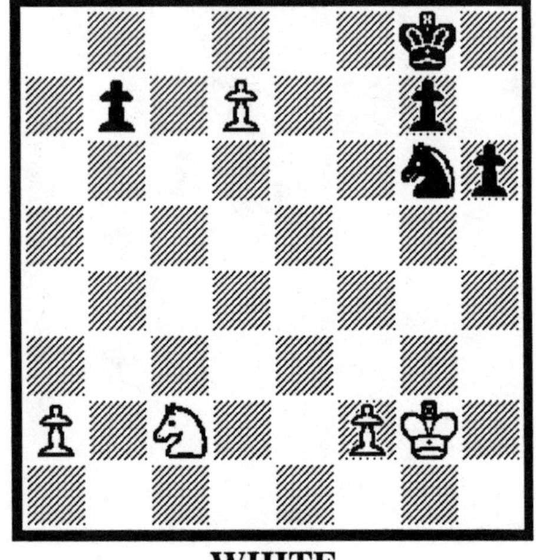

WHITE

It is Black's turn to move. White's advanced pawn is only one square from promoting. Black's king is too far away to do anything about it. But there is a two move plan that enables Black's knight to control the pawn's promotion square. What should Black's next two moves be?

Don't read the hint until you've tried your best.

Answer on page 114

(Hint: The first move is a check.)

PUZZLE #81

It is Black's turn to move. White is ready to play "knight takes pawn," but Black has one way to prevent it. How?

Confused? Read "About the Puzzles" starting on page 2.

Answer on page 115

PUZZLE #82

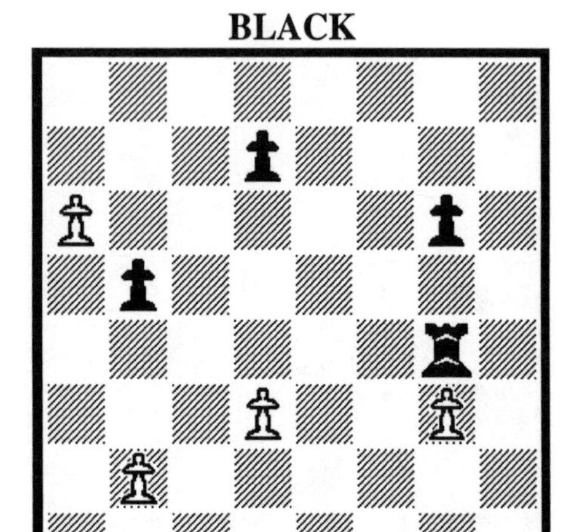

It is White's turn to move. White has a pawn only two squares from promoting. How can White promote that pawn so that Black's rook can't capture the promoted piece?

Confused? Read "About the Puzzles" starting on page 2.

Answer on page 116

PUZZLE #83

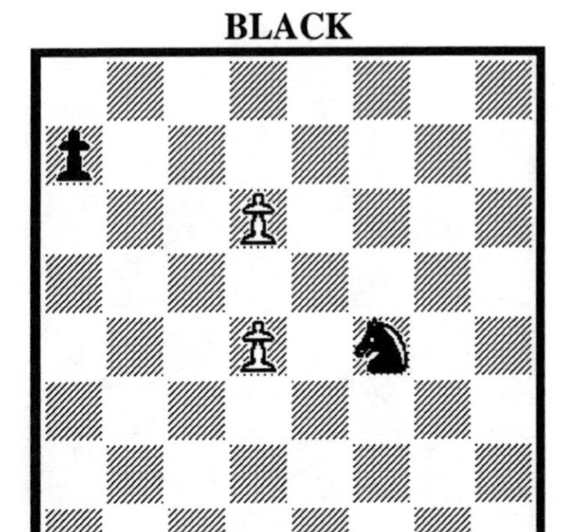

It is White's turn to move. White has a way to promote in a few moves so that Black's knight can't capture the promoted piece. How?

Don't read the hint until you've tried your best.

Answer on page 117

(Hint: Think where the knight needs to go to capture the new promoted piece. Then find a way to capture the knight if it goes to that square.)

PUZZLE #84

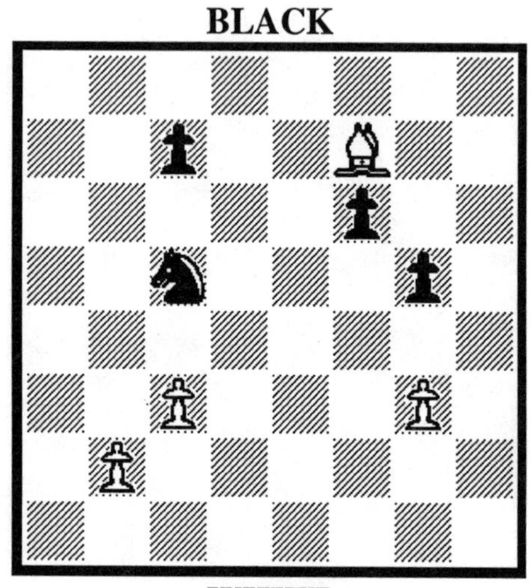

It is Black's turn to move. Black has a way to win at least a pawn no matter what White does. What move should Black play?

Confused? Read "About the Puzzles" starting on page 2.

Answer on page 118

PUZZLE #85

BLACK

WHITE

It is White's turn to move. If White plays "bishop takes pawn," then Black can reply "bishop takes pawn." Yet there is a way for White to win a pawn on the next move. What move should White play?

Don't read the hint until you've tried your best.

Answer on page 119

(Hint: Stop Black from playing "bishop takes pawn.")

PUZZLE #86

WHITE

It is Black's turn to move. White's king and queen are moving in on Black's king. But Black has a way to get a draw by stalemate. How?

Confused? Read "About the Puzzles" starting on page 2.

Answer on page 120

PUZZLE #87

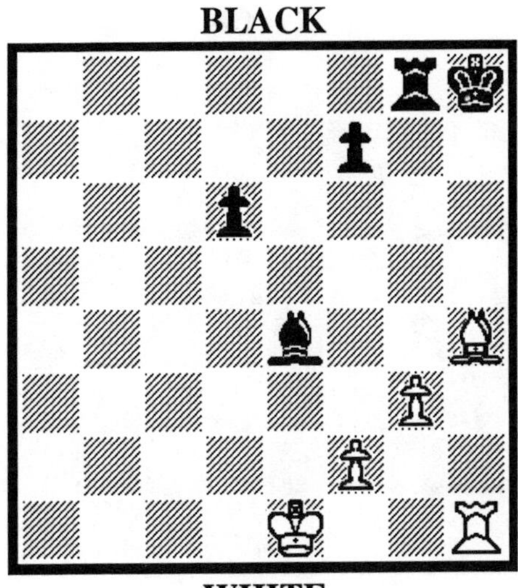

It is White's turn to move. White can checkmate Black in one move. Can you find it?

Confused? Read "About the Puzzles" starting on page 2.

Answer on page 121

PUZZLE #88

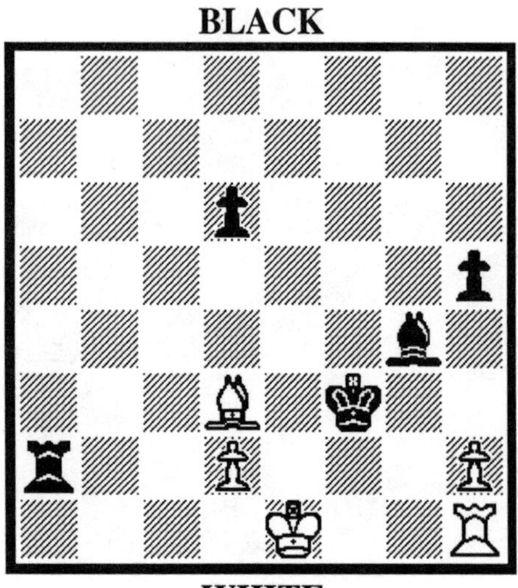

It is White's turn to move. White can checkmate Black in one move. Can you find it?

Confused? Read "About the Puzzles" starting on page 2.

Answer on page 122

PUZZLE #89

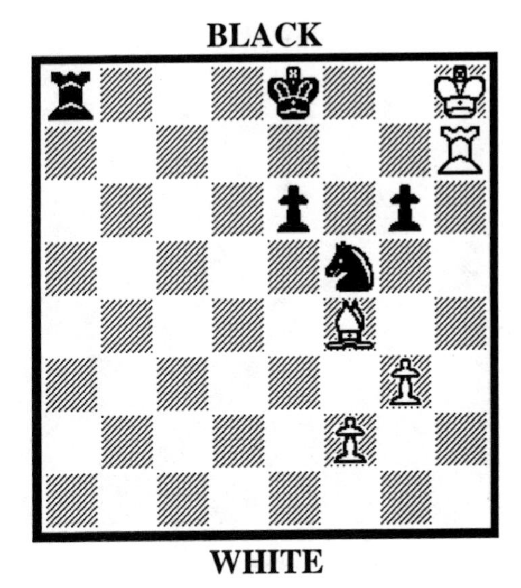

It is Black's turn to move. Black can checkmate White in one move. Can you find it?

Confused? Read "About the Puzzles" starting on page 2.

Answer on page 123

PUZZLE #90

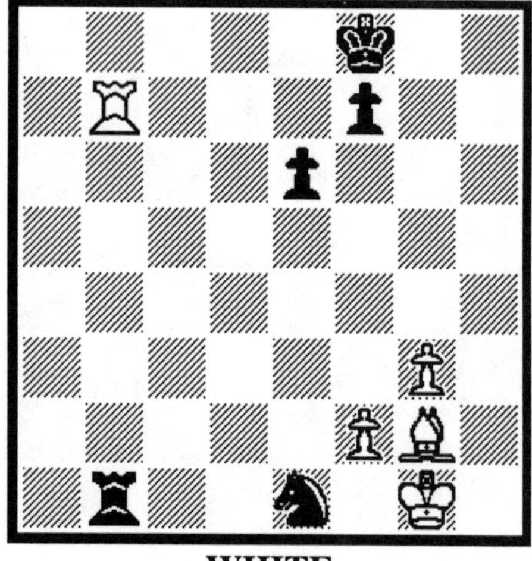

It is Black's turn to move. Black can checkmate White in one move. Can you find it?

Confused? Read "About the Puzzles" starting on page 2.

Answer on page 124

ANSWERS

PUZZLE #1

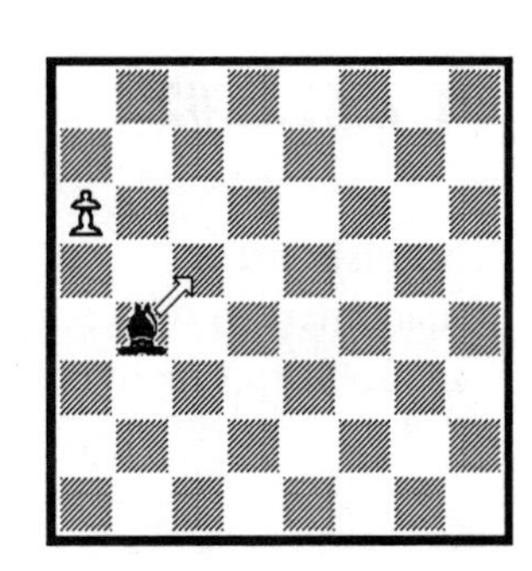

PUZZLE #31

Black's next move will be to put the rook on the square marked with an "x". Then it can capture the promoted piece.

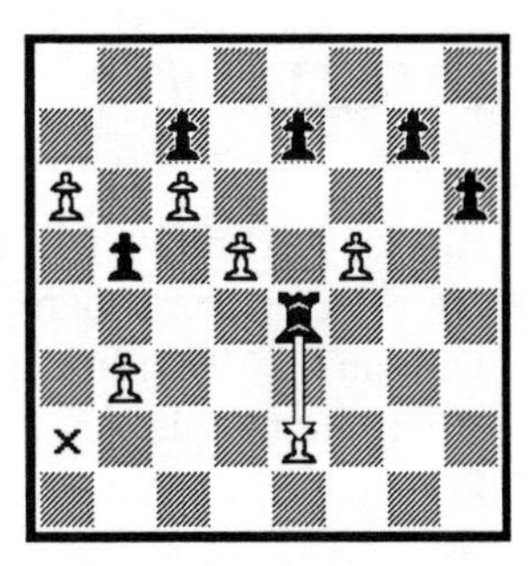

PUZZLE #61

PUZZLE #2

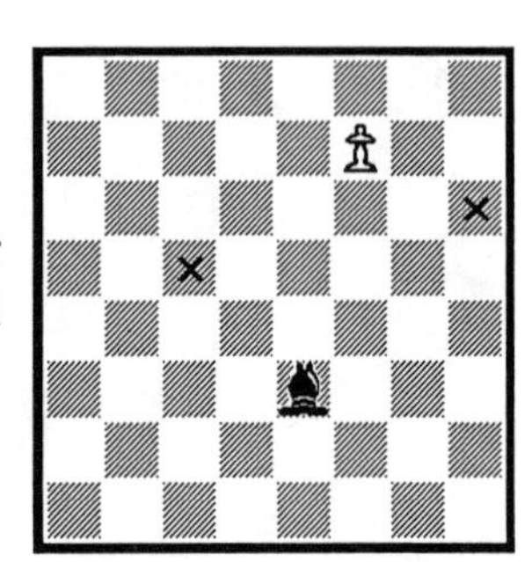

The bishop can move to either square marked with an "x", and capture the promoted piece.

PUZZLE #32

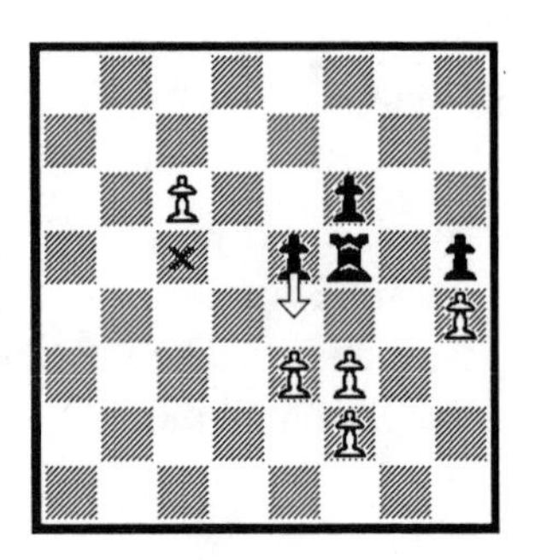

Black's next move will be to put the rook on the square marked with an "x". Then it can capture the promoted piece.

PUZZLE #62

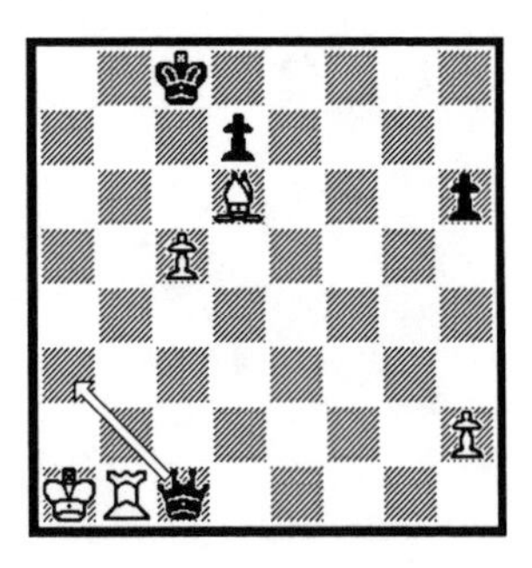

PUZZLE #3

PUZZLE #33

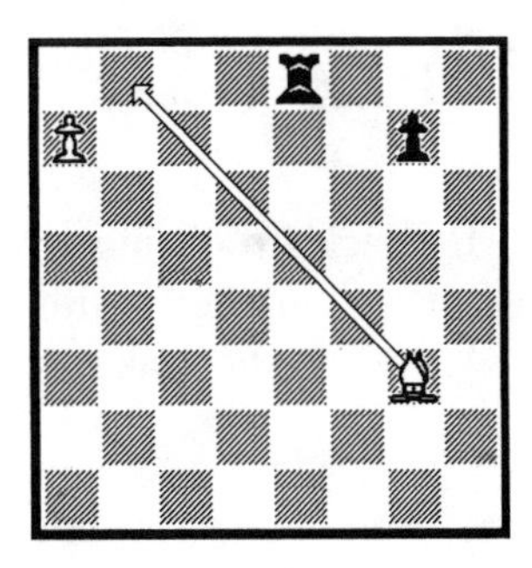

PUZZLE #63

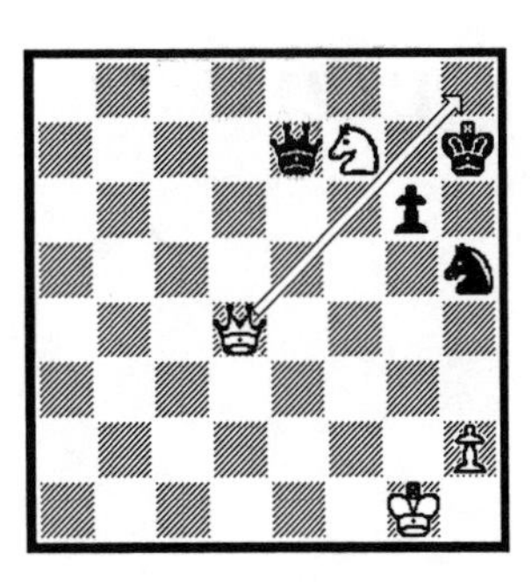

PUZZLE #4

First the bishop moves to the square marked with an "x". On its next move, the bishop goes to the square marked with a "z".

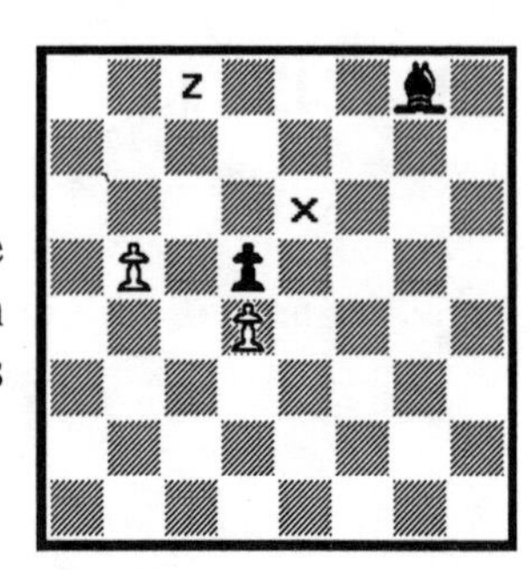

PUZZLE #34

If Black's rook moves to either square marked with an "x", White's bishop takes it.

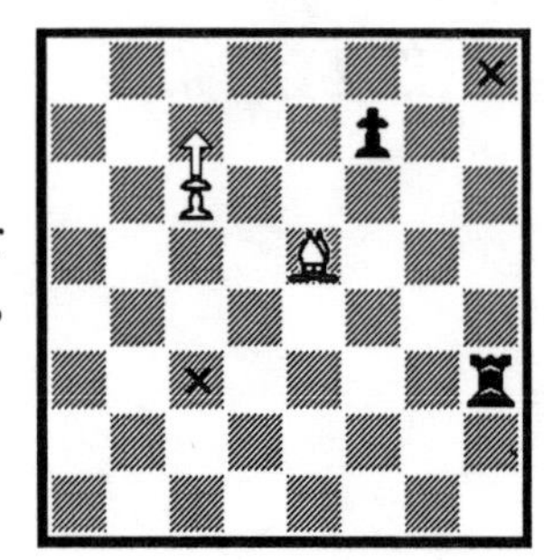

PUZZLE #64

PUZZLE #5

First the bishop moves to the square marked with an "x". On its next move, the bishop goes to the square marked with a "z".

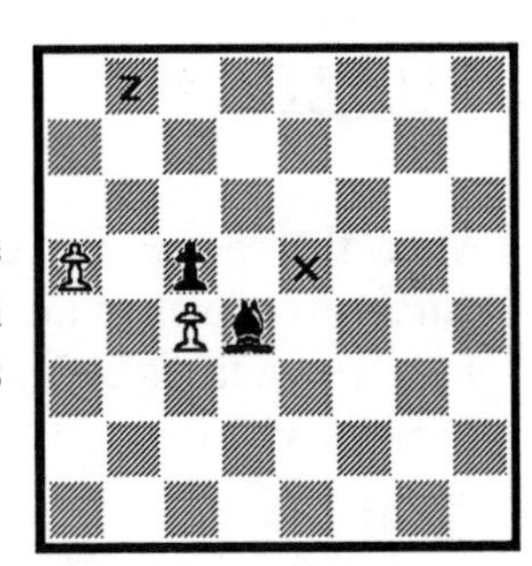

PUZZLE #35

If Black now plays "rook takes bishop," White can play "pawn takes rook."

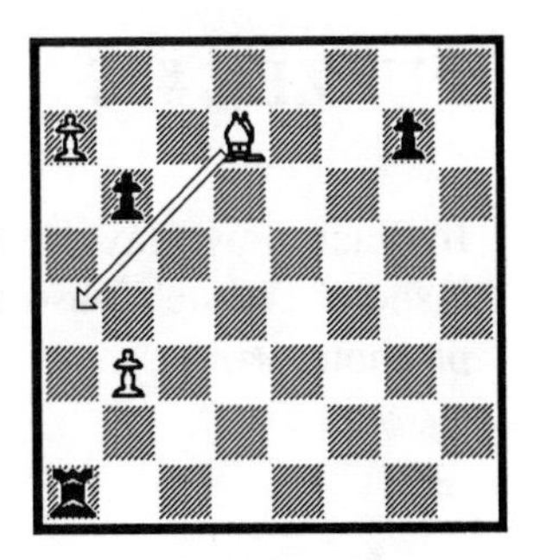

PUZZLE #65

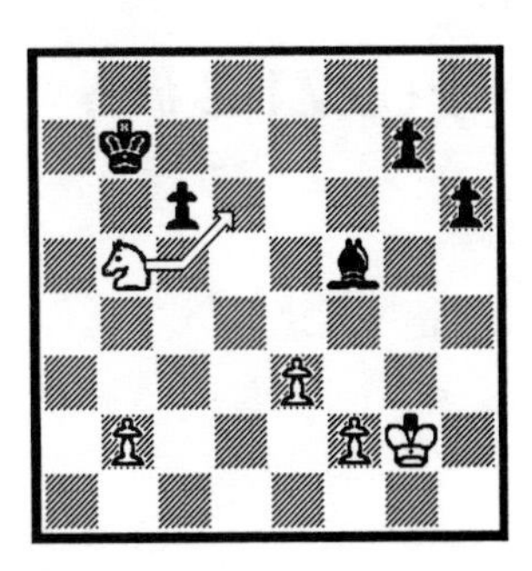

PUZZLE #6

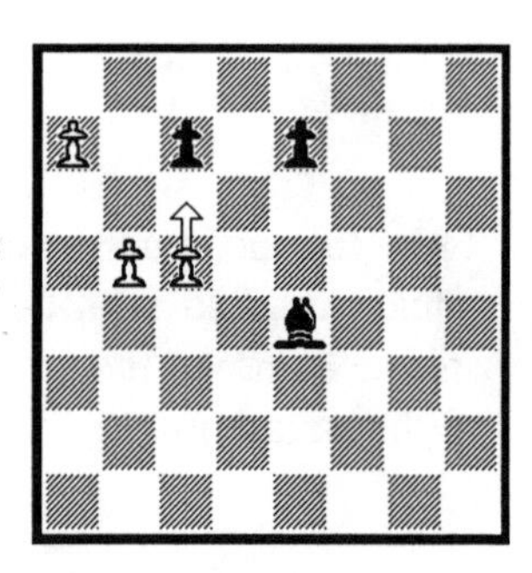

After this pawn move, White can answer "bishop takes pawn" with "pawn takes bishop."

PUZZLE #36

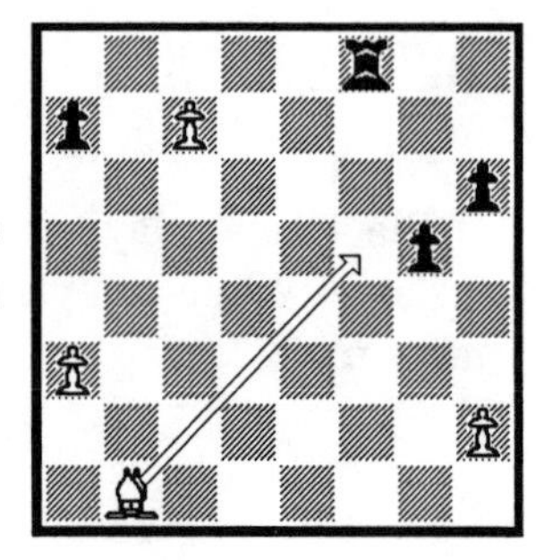

If Black now plays "rook takes bishop," White's passed pawn promotes safely.

PUZZLE #66

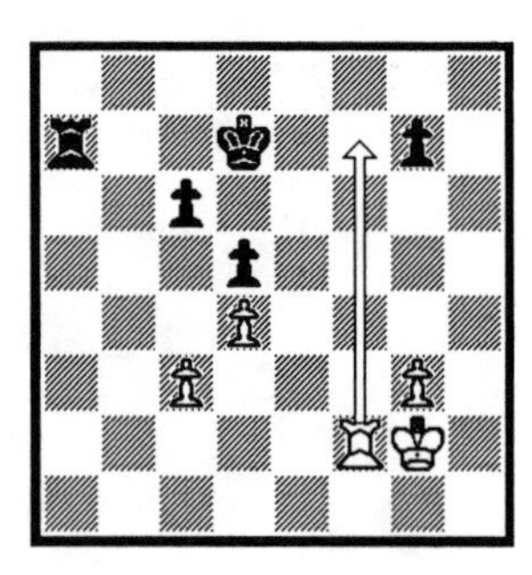

PUZZLE #7

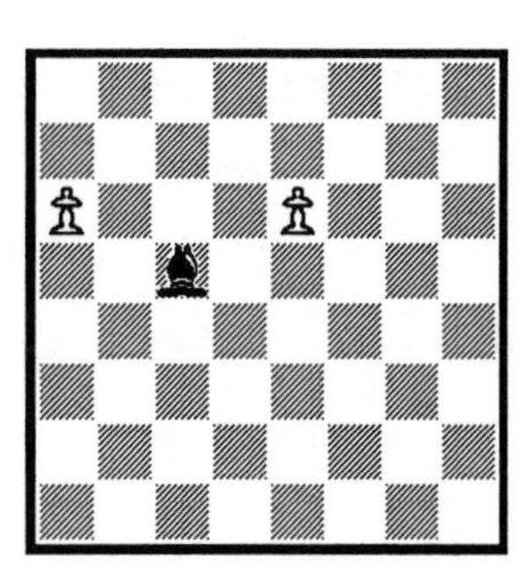

White can promote by moving either pawn! If Black's bishop takes it, the other pawn promotes.

PUZZLE #37

PUZZLE #67

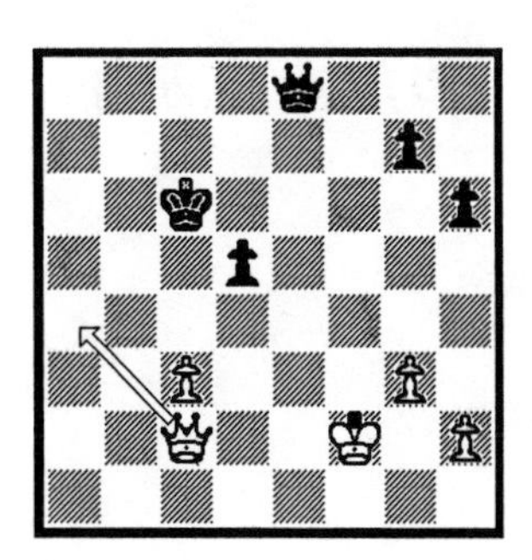

PUZZLE #8

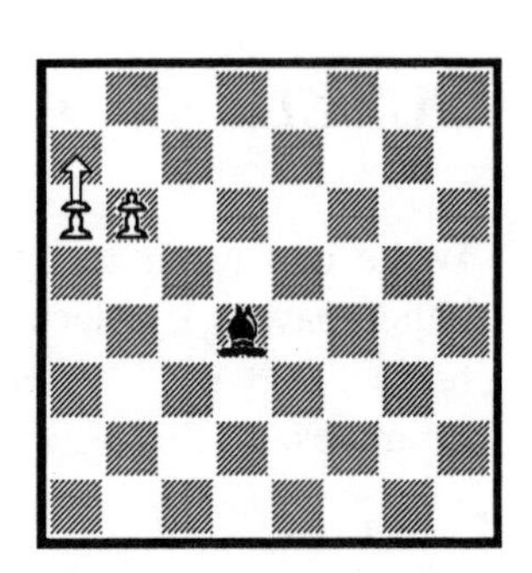

PUZZLE #38

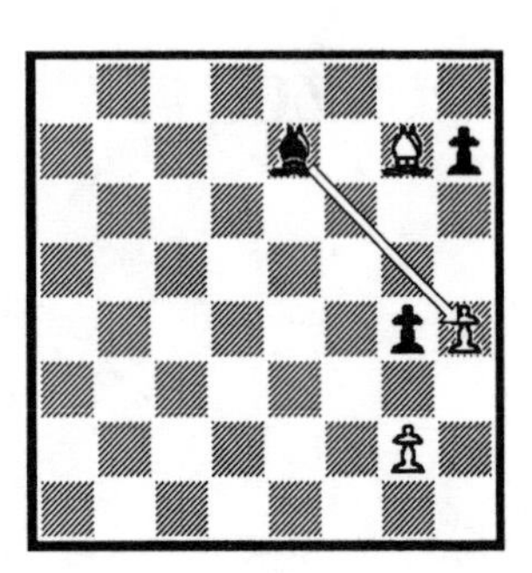

PUZZLE #68

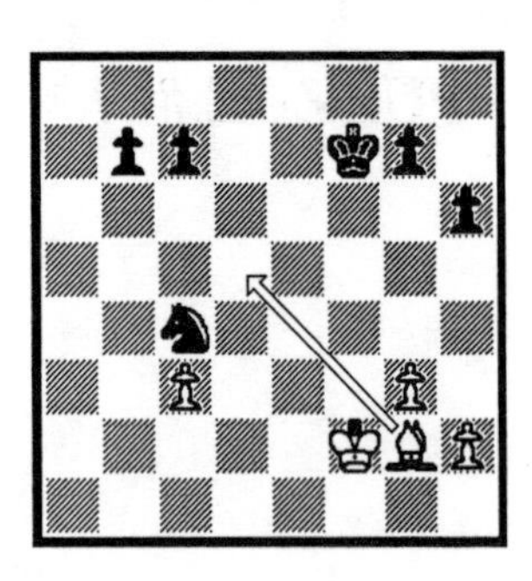

PUZZLE #9

PUZZLE #39

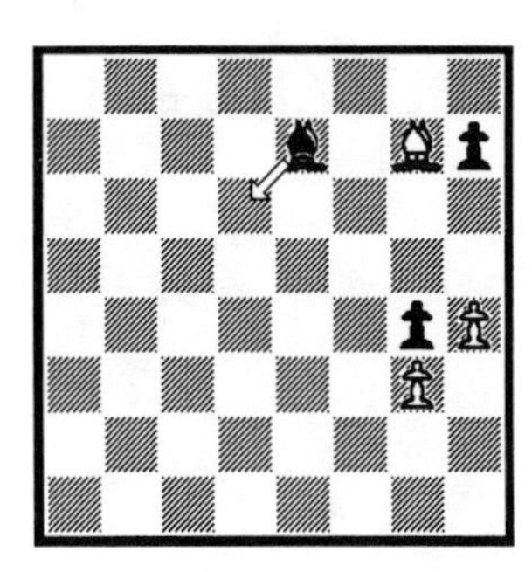

PUZZLE #69

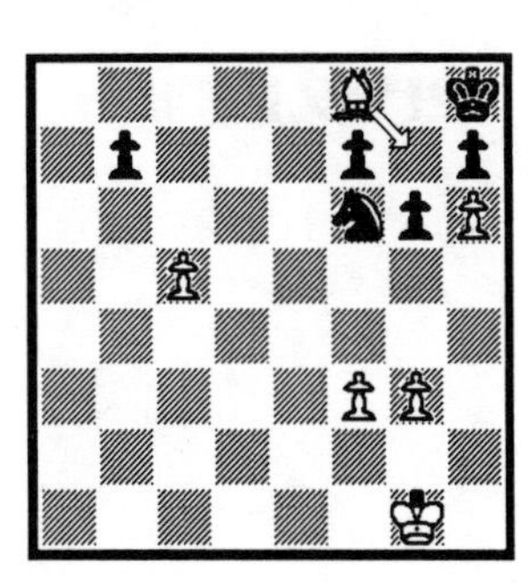

PUZZLE #10

PUZZLE #40

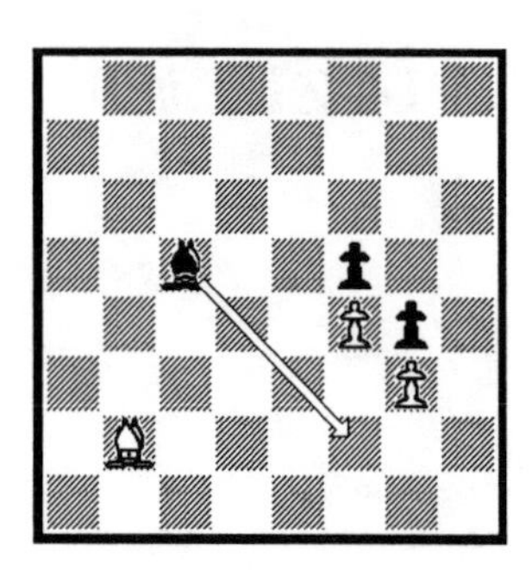

PUZZLE #70

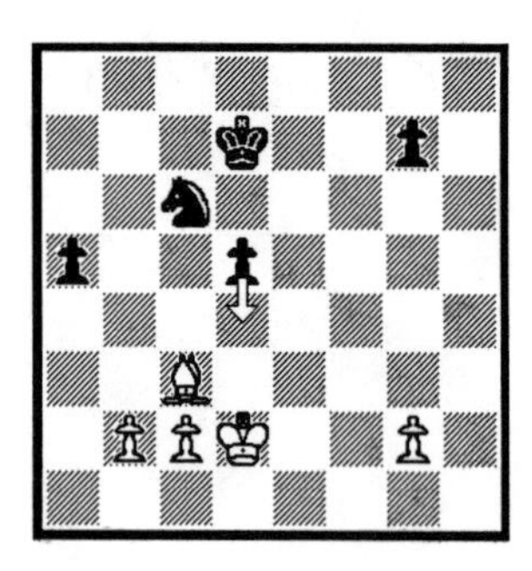

PUZZLE #11

PUZZLE #41

Now White's bishop must move, and Black will play "bishop takes pawn."

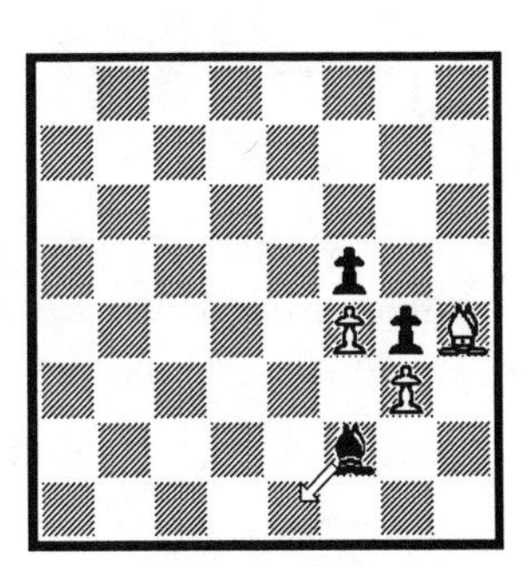

PUZZLE #71

Black can't play "king takes pawn" because the pawn is protected by White's bishop.

PUZZLE #12

Black's knight moves to the square marked by an "x".

PUZZLE #42

Black's bishop will move to where this pawn was, then to the square marked with an "x".

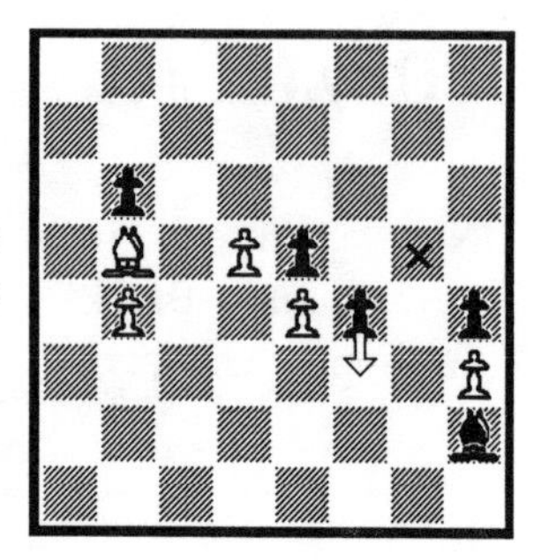

PUZZLE #72

Black's king must move, and White will play "king takes knight."

PUZZLE #13

If Black takes this pawn, White's other pawn will promote. If Black doesn't take the pawn, White will keep moving it.

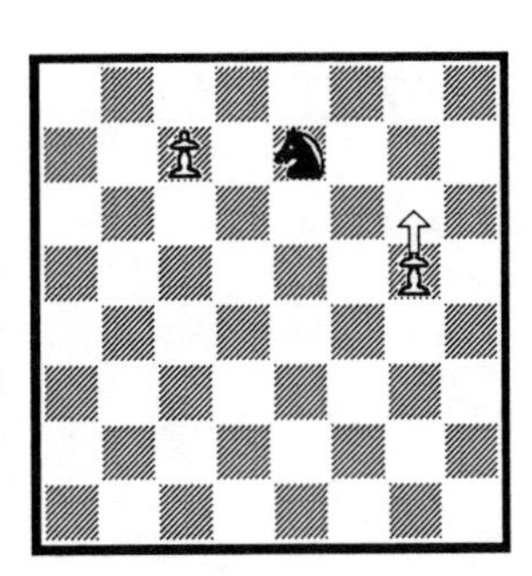

PUZZLE #43

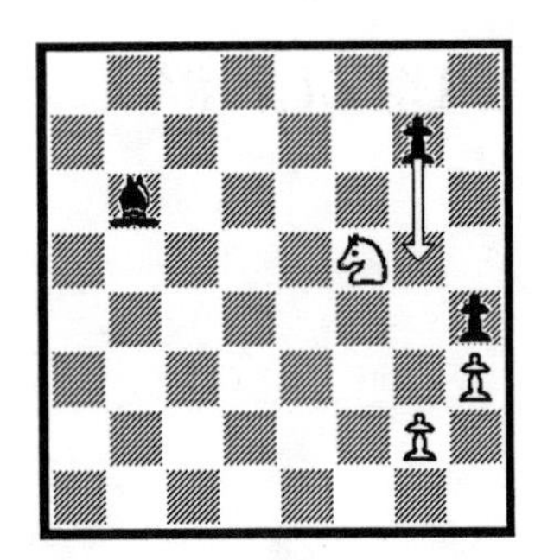

PUZZLE #73

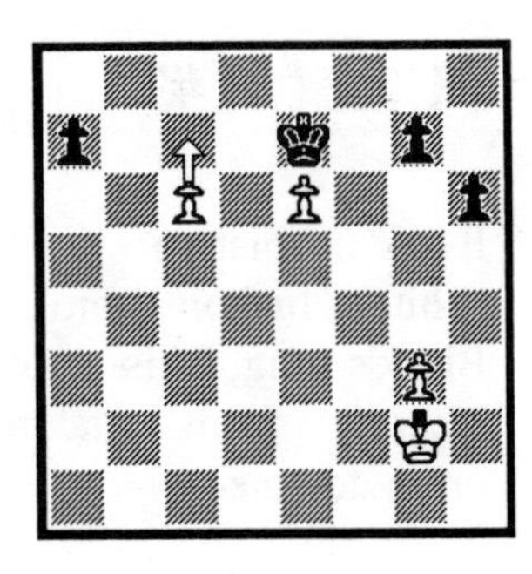

PUZZLE #14

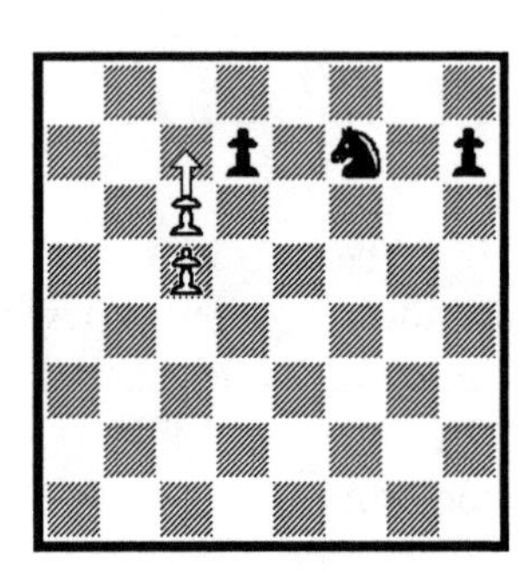

PUZZLE #44

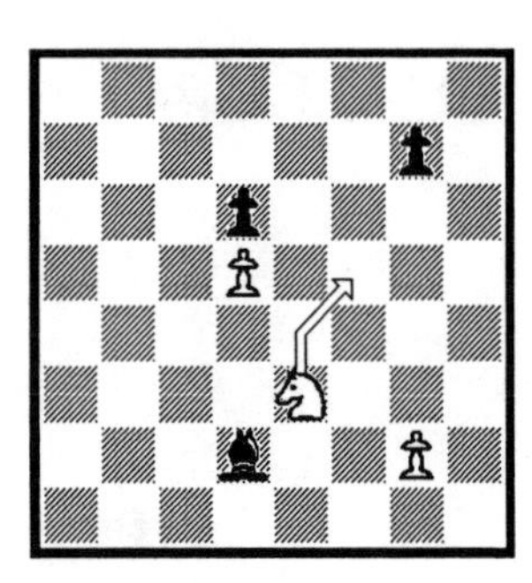

PUZZLE #74

Black's bishop must keep White's bishop from checking Black's king. This stops Black's bishop from taking the promoted piece.

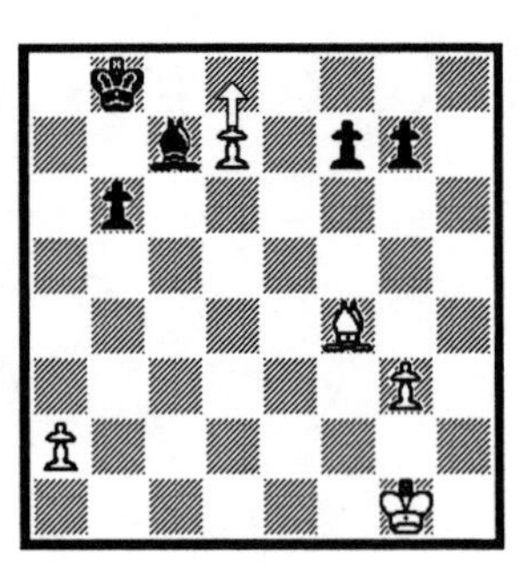

PUZZLE #15

PUZZLE #45

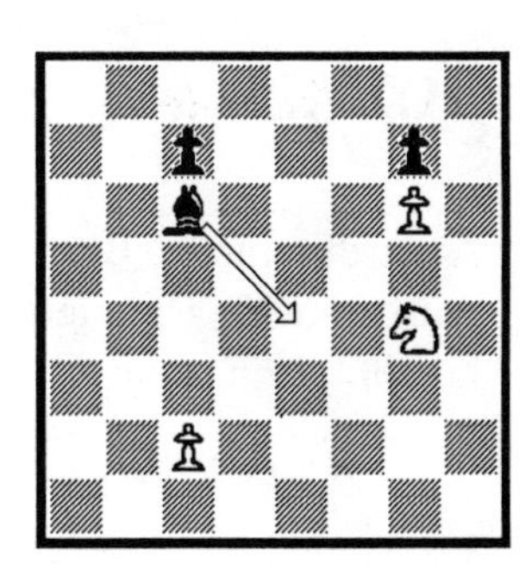

PUZZLE #75

White's next move will be with the pawn, checkmate!

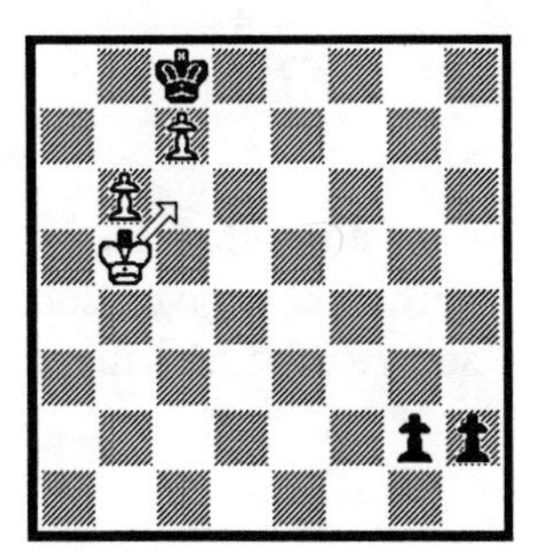

PUZZLE #16

Black's knight will now be able to go where this pawn was.

PUZZLE #46

After this move, Black's bishop must move. This lets White's knight take a pawn for free.

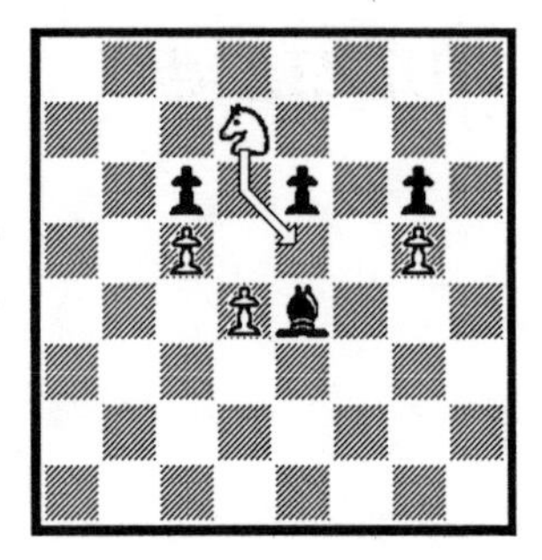

PUZZLE #76

To stop the check, Black's knight must give itself up on the square marked with an "x".

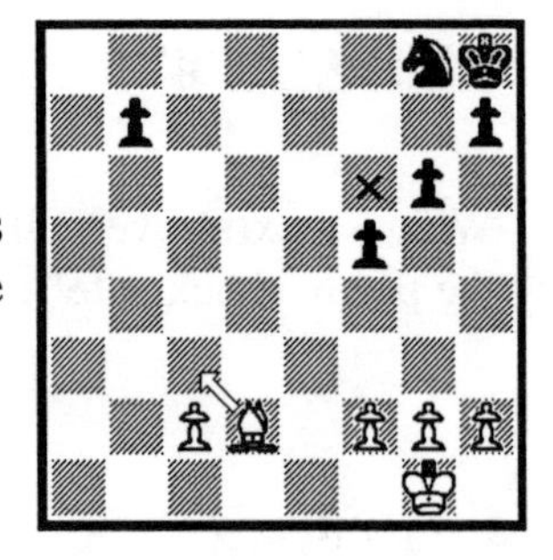

PUZZLE #17

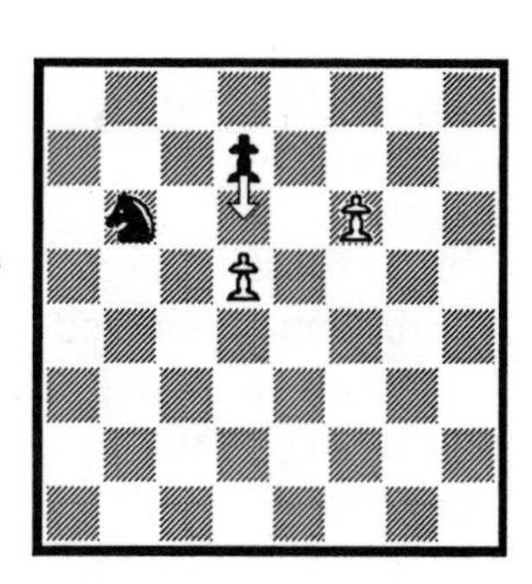

Black's knight will now be able to go where this pawn was.

PUZZLE #47

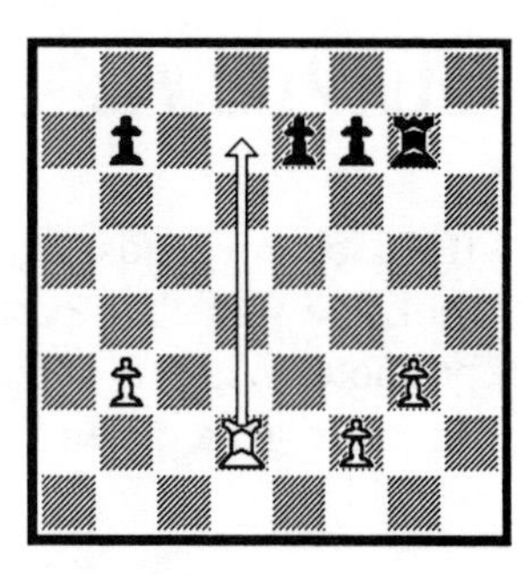

PUZZLE #77

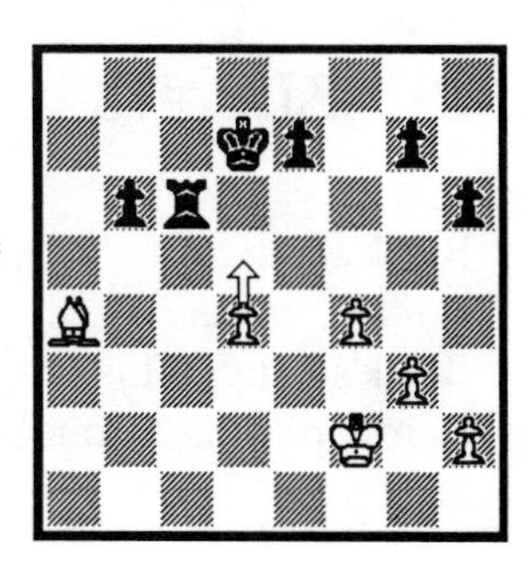

Next move, White takes the rook for free.

PUZZLE #18

First, Black's knight will move to the square marked by an "x". On its next move, the knight will move to the square marked by a "z".

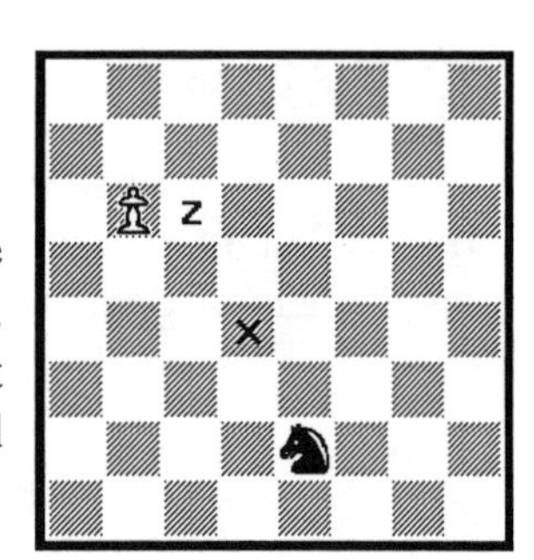

PUZZLE #48

If Black responds "rook takes rook," White's pawn will promote. White is happy to lose a rook to get a queen.

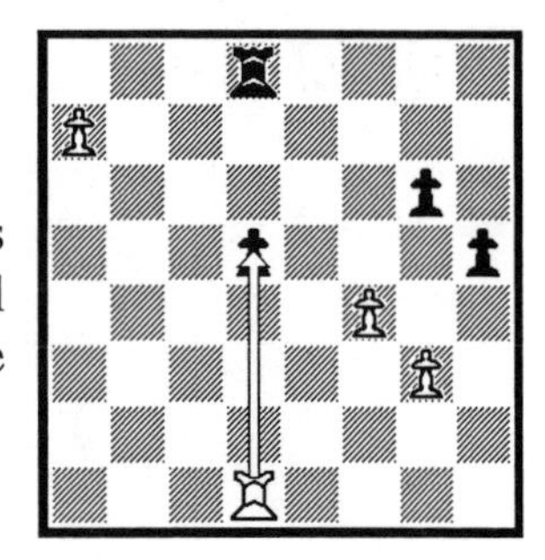

PUZZLE #78

Black's queen must keep White's queen from checking Black's king. This stops Black from playing "queen takes bishop."

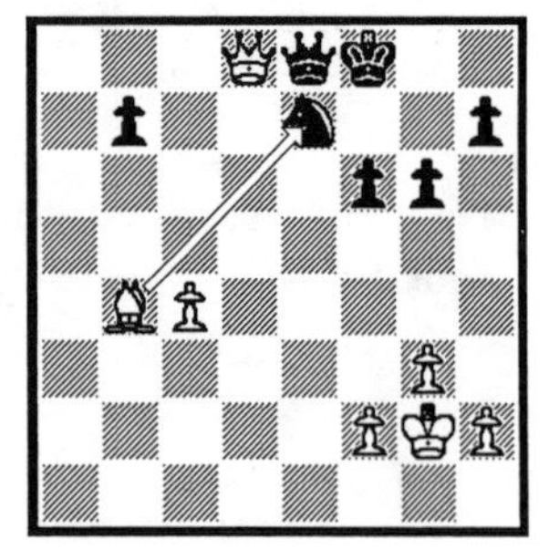

PUZZLE #19

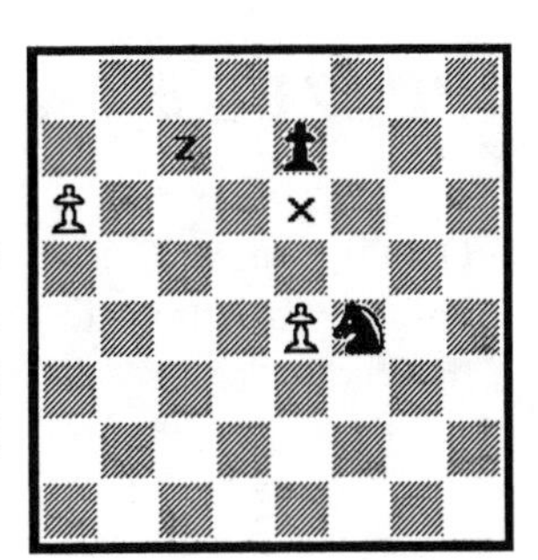

First, Black's knight will move to the square marked by an "x". On its next move, the knight will move to the square marked by a "z".

PUZZLE #49

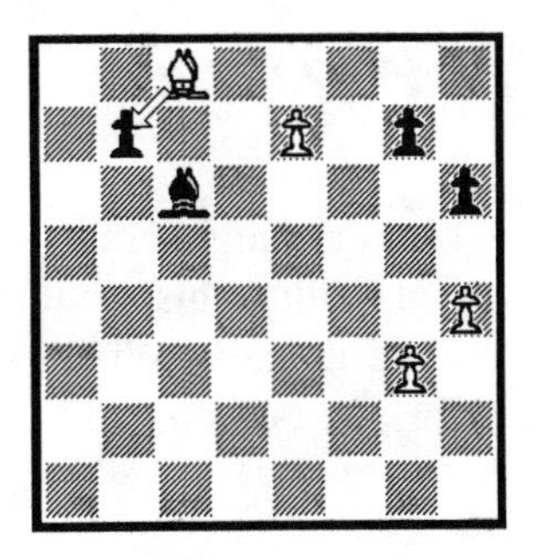

If Black responds "bishop takes bishop," White's pawn will promote. White is happy to lose a bishop to get a queen.

PUZZLE #79

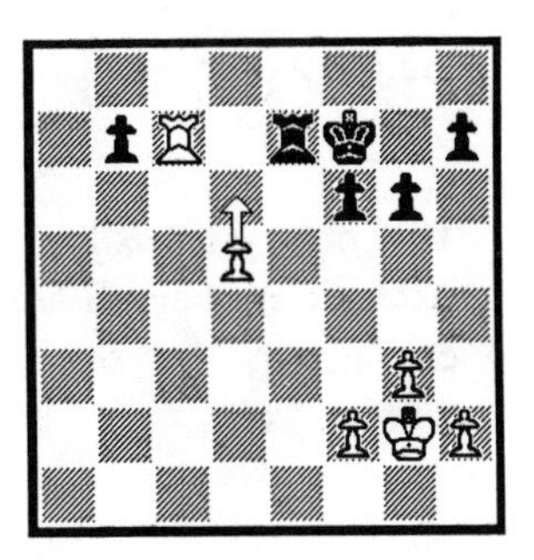

Black's rook has no good move. If Black plays "rook takes rook," White plays "pawn takes rook" and then promotes.

PUZZLE #20

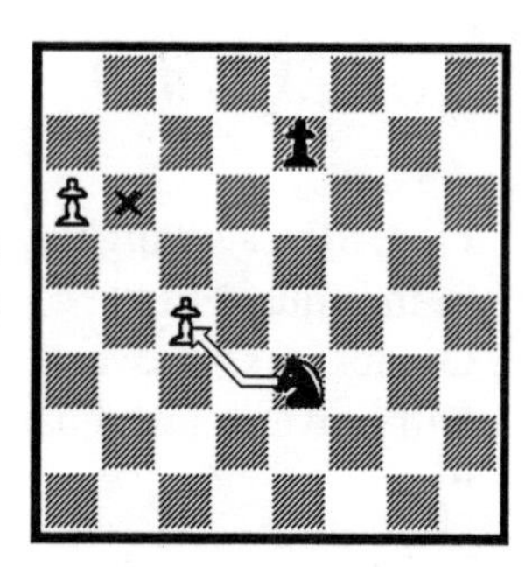

On its next move, Black's knight will move to the square marked by an "x".

PUZZLE #50

Black's knight must move so that White's bishop doesn't take it. But then White can play "bishop takes pawn."

PUZZLE #80

This puts White's king in check. After it moves, Black's knight can go to the square marked with an "x".

PUZZLE #21

Now anywhere the knight goes, a White pawn will take it.

PUZZLE #51

If Black's bishop moves to either square marked with an "x", the knight will take it. Otherwise White can take a pawn for free.

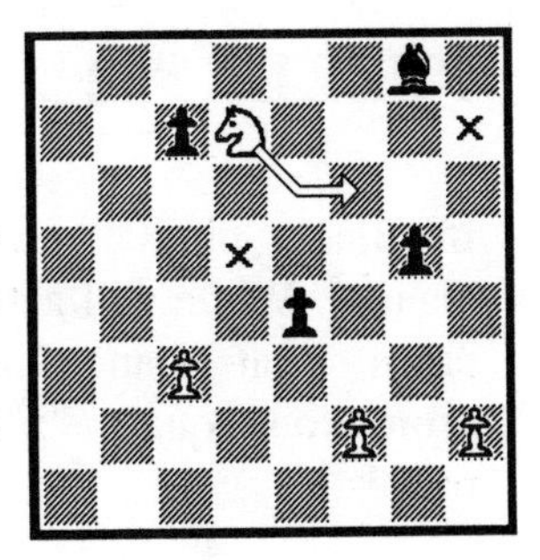

PUZZLE #81

PUZZLE #22

Black's knight has no way to stop White's advanced pawn from promoting. Try it!

PUZZLE #52

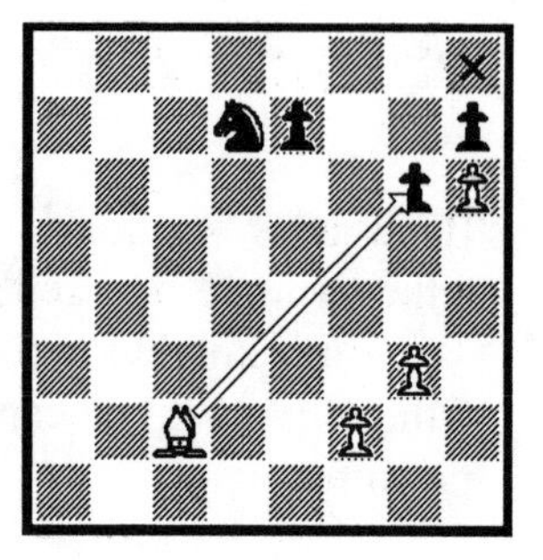

If Black plays "pawn takes bishop," White will get a passed pawn that can reach the promotion square "x" in two moves.

PUZZLE #82

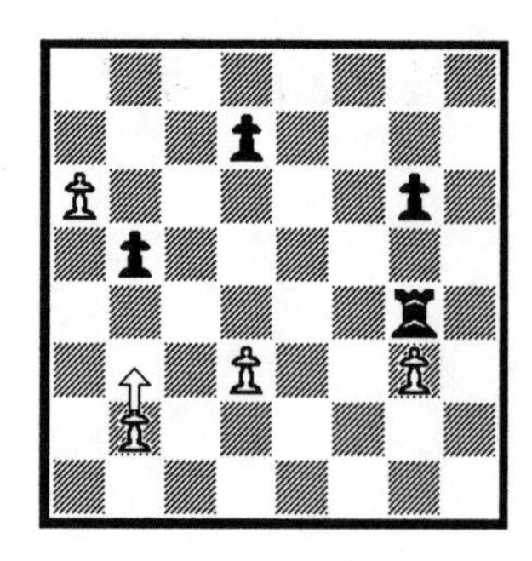

PUZZLE #23

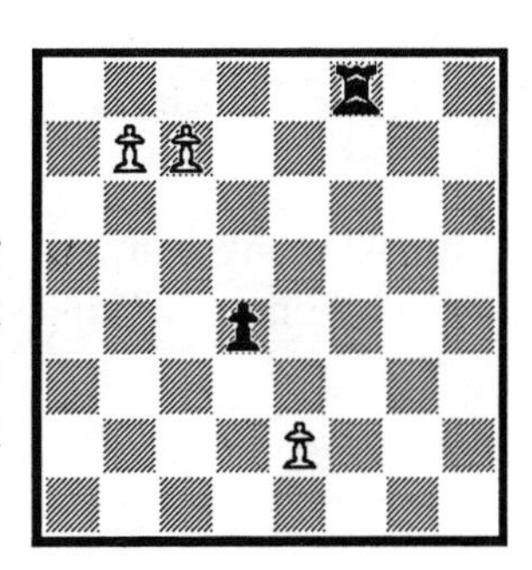

White can promote either passed pawn! If Black's rook takes the promoted piece, the other pawn can take the rook and promote.

PUZZLE #53

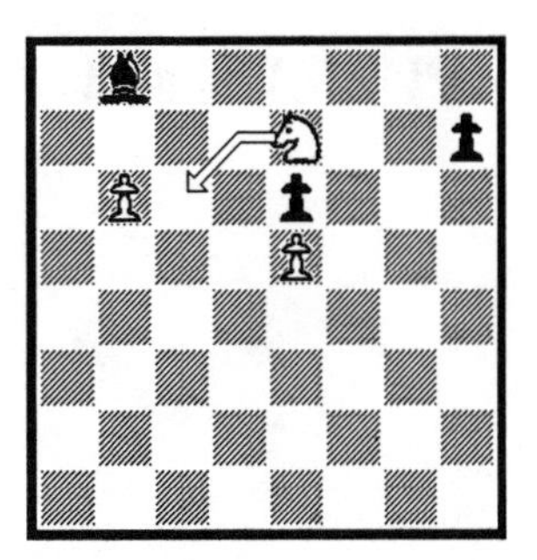

If Black now plays "bishop takes pawn," White plays "knight takes bishop."

PUZZLE #83

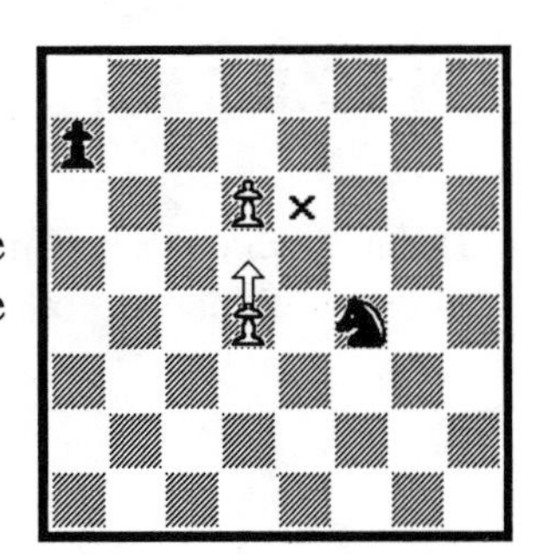

Now if the knight moves to the square marked by an "x", the pawn can take it.

PUZZLE #24

Black's rook can only stop one pawn from promoting safely.

PUZZLE #54

PUZZLE #84

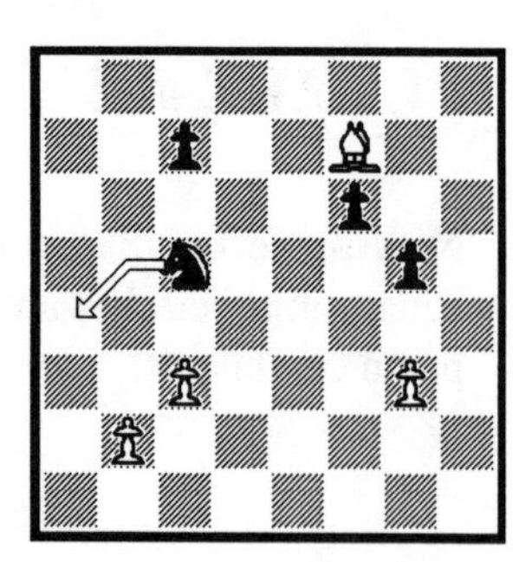

If the attacked pawn moves, the knight will take the other pawn.

PUZZLE #25

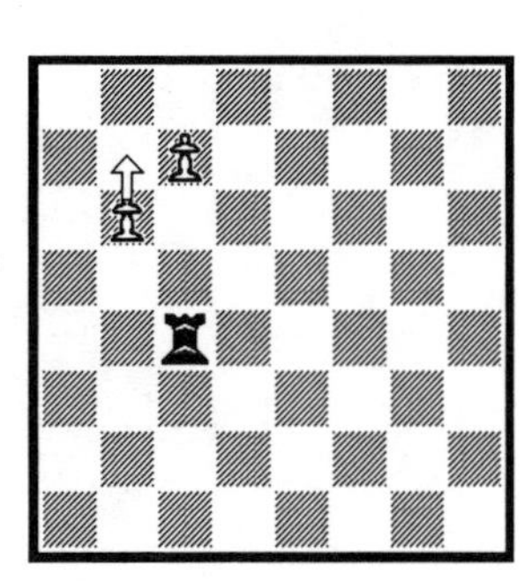

Once again, the pawns are too much for the rook.

PUZZLE #55

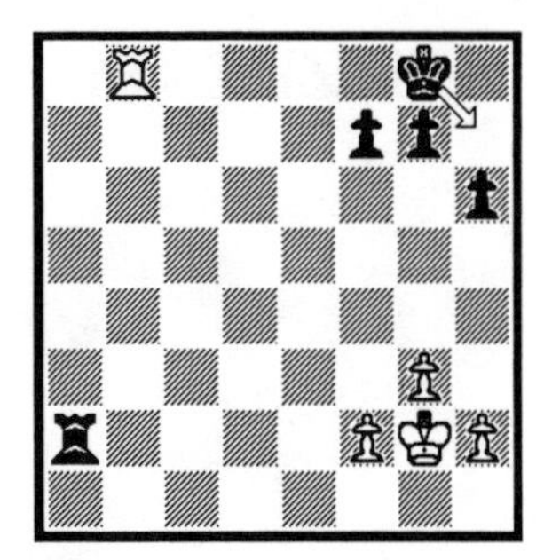

PUZZLE #85

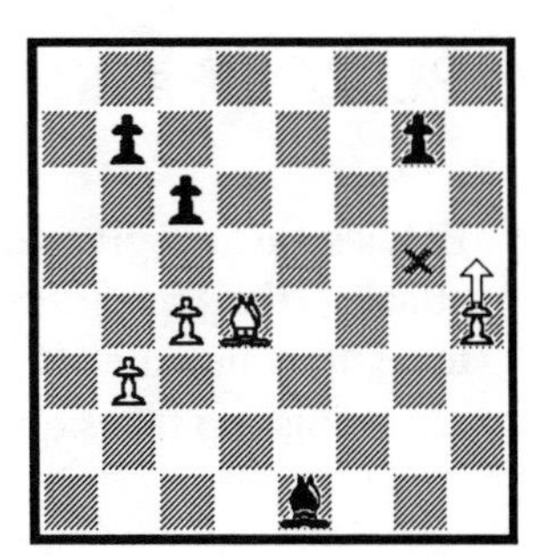

If Black's pawn now moves to the square marked by an "x", White's pawn can capture it "en passant."

PUZZLE #26

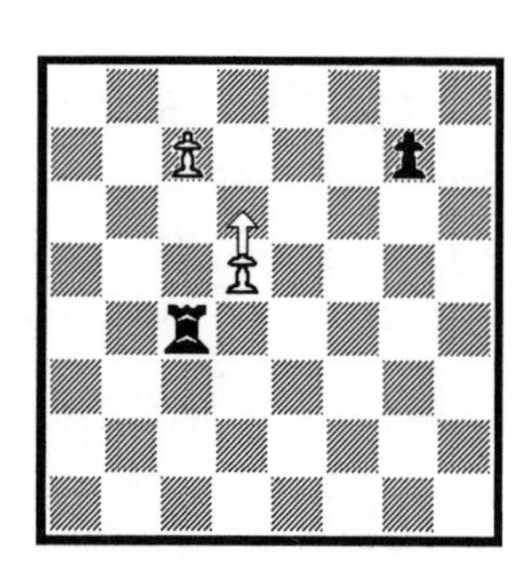

PUZZLE #56

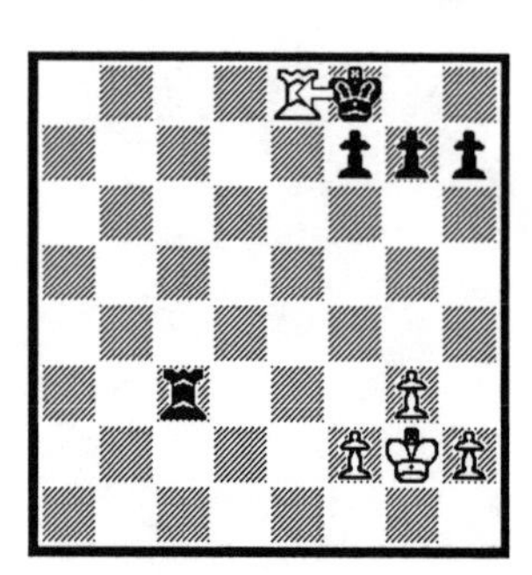

PUZZLE #86

Black's bishop gives check and attacks the queen. If White takes it, stalemate! If not, Black plays "bishop takes queen."

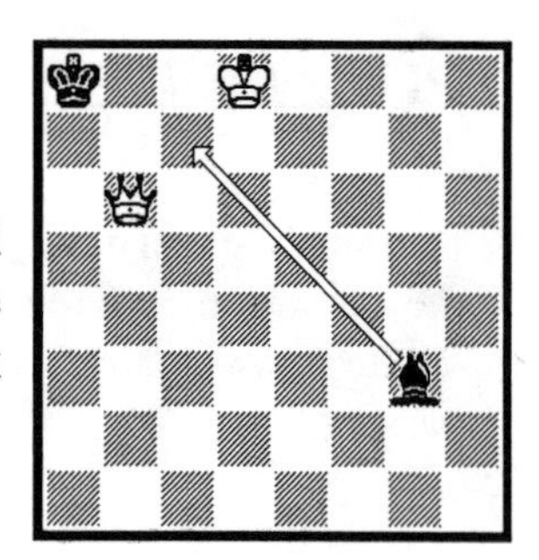

PUZZLE #27

PUZZLE #57

Black stops the check by moving the knight to the square marked with an "x".

PUZZLE #87

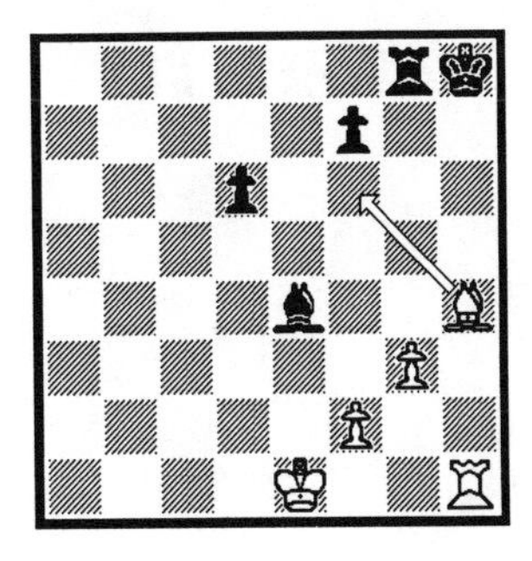

PUZZLE #28

If Black's rook takes this pawn, White's other passed pawn promotes. If Black doesn't take the pawn, it will keep moving.

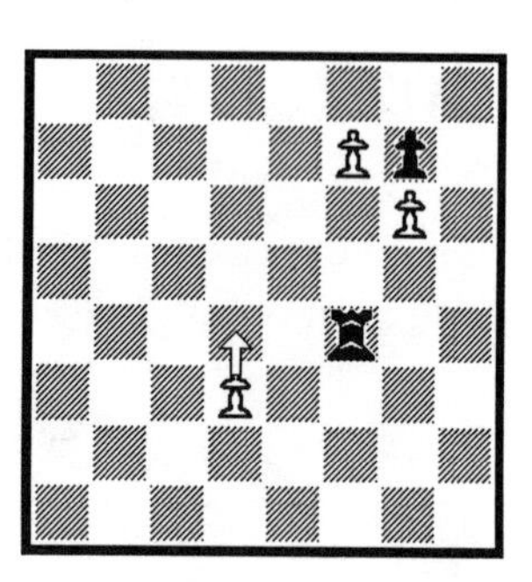

PUZZLE #58

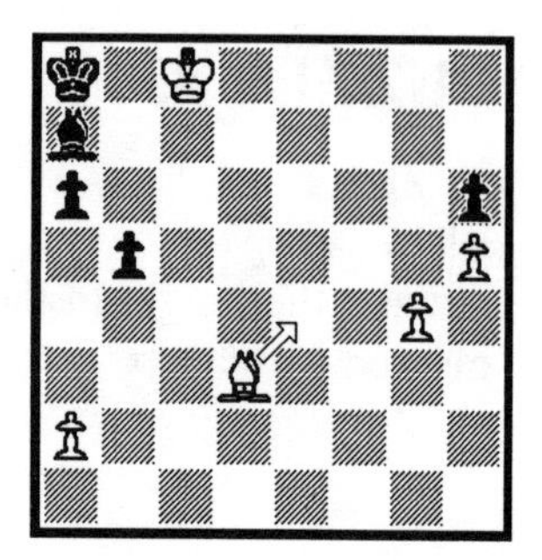

PUZZLE #88

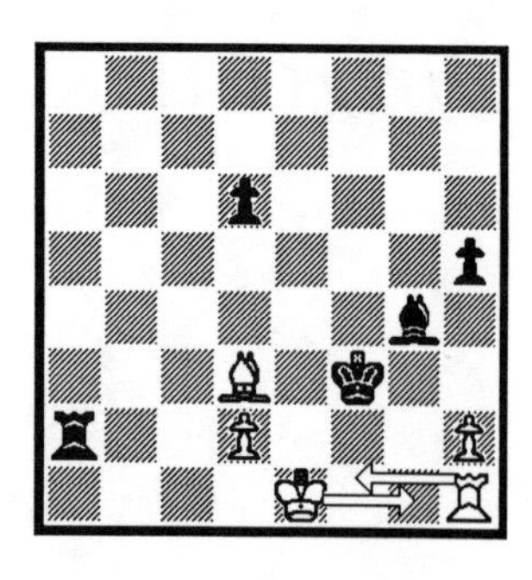

PUZZLE #29

Now the rook can watch the promotion square of each pawn.

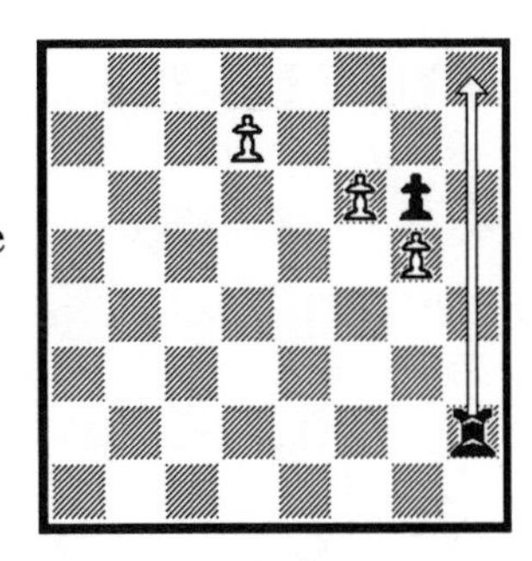

PUZZLE #59

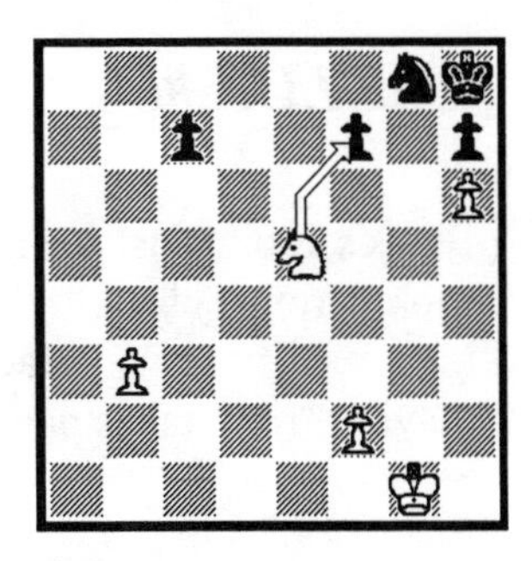

PUZZLE #89

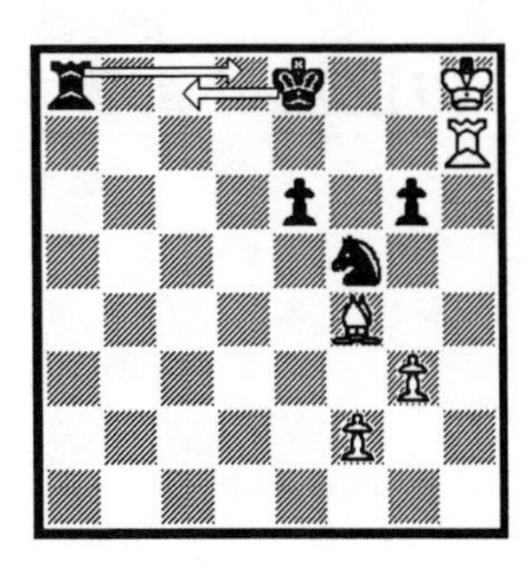

PUZZLE #30

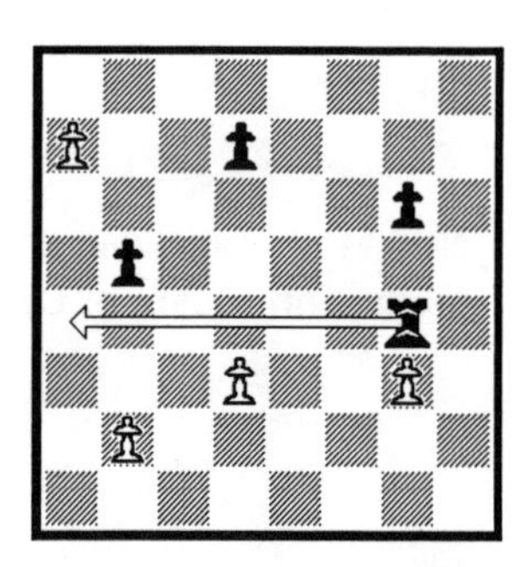

PUZZLE #60

Black's rook must keep White's rook from checking Black's king. This stops Black from playing "rook takes pawn."

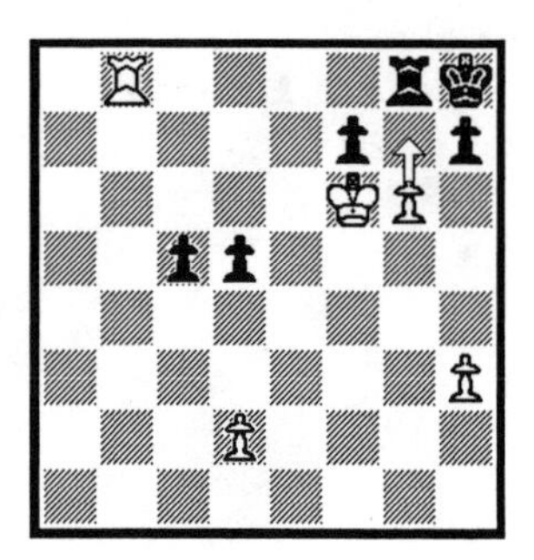

PUZZLE #90

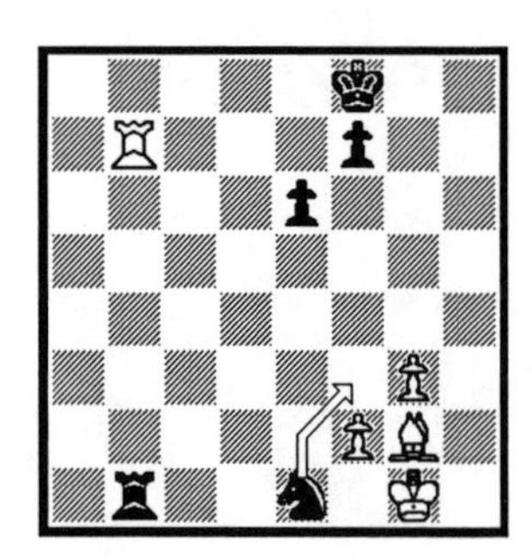